DEVELOPING AND IMPLEMENTING A WHOLE-SCHOOL BEHAVIOUR POLICY

A Practical Approach

Edited by

DON CLARKE
AND ANNE MURRAY

David Fulton Publishers

David Fulton Publishers Ltd
2 Barbon Close, London WC1N 3JX

First published in Great Britain by
David Fulton publishers Ltd 1996
Reprinted 1998

Note: The right of the authors to be identified as the authors of this work has been asserted by them in accordance with the Copyright, Designs and Patents Act 1988.

Copyright © The London Borough of Tower Hamlets;
Support for Learning Service

British Library Cataloguing in Publication Data

A catalogue record for this book is available from the British Library

ISBN 1-85346-365-5

Typeset by Don Clarke
Printed in Great Britain by Bell and Bain Ltd, Glasgow.

Contents

Acknowledgements

This book grew out of the work done by a group of teachers in the Tower Hamlets Support for Learning Service who had part of their time funded by GEST. The 'GEST team' worked in schools supporting them in the development of behaviour polices.

The GEST team at the time of publication were Harry Ayers, Don Clarke, Warwick Dyer, Alastair Ross, Francesca Gray, Peggy Gosling, Bob Minter, Anne Murray and Fiona Stephen. Sarah Cooper and Irene Ware were members of the team when much of the work was done. Anne Murray was the manager of the project.

We are indebted to all the schools in which we worked and we thank them for the privilege of working with them.

We would like to thank the other teachers and headteachers who have been supportive of the process.

Thanks also to Bill Rogers who provided much inspiration.

We would particularly like to express our thanks to Liz Vickerie (Director) and Specialist Teachers of the *Tower Hamlets Support for Learning Service* for their encouragement as well as their tolerance with the over-use of the limited IT resources.

Special thanks to:

Su Edwards at Rosendale Junior School in Lambeth for her support and contributions to the sheets.

Penny Bentley for her permission to use the conflict resolution technique used at Columbia School in Tower Hamlets

The pupils at Cayley School in Tower Hamlets for their drawings

Created on *Acorn 'A' series* and *'Risc PC'* computers
Materials designed using *ArtWorks* from *Computer Concepts*
DeskTop Published using *Impression Publisher* from *Computer Concepts*

About this book

This book gathers together some of the experience of a group of Tower Hamlets SLS teachers who have worked in collaboration with mainstream colleagues to develop whole-school behaviour policies.

It aims to present key issues related to developing behaviour policies and to provide useful materials and ideas which can be used by schools as starting points for their own projects.

The chapters can be read independently of one another and so the reader can feel free to 'dip in' as needs or interest demands. To this end, there is some overlap between chapters which has been retained.

About the contributors

Don Clarke focuses on:
- Why have a behaviour policy?
- What needs to go into the policy?
- Issues which can be usefully considered when developing a policy
- Some strategies which support a whole school approach to managing behaviour

Peggy Gosling, Anne Murray and Fiona Stephen discuss some organisational change aspects of policy development as well as the issue of developing consensus.

Alastair Ross suggests strategies and structures for enabling the whole school community to effectively contribute to the process of behaviour policy-making.

Francesca Gray discusses assessment and information gathering including:
- The facts – which can be observed, monitored and recorded
- People's perceptions – staff, pupils', parents' and other members of the school community

Alastair Ross' second chapter draws on his experience of developing policies in primary schools.

Harry Ayers discusses some of the issues arising out of the development of behaviour policies in secondary schools. In particular he identifies some of the factors which can impede the process of effective policy development.

Although the last two authors focus on particular phases, there are far more similarities than differences in the processes and so the reader, what ever phase they are concerned with, could benefit from the material in both sections.

No policy is complete without a process of monitoring and evaluating its effectiveness. **Peggy Gosling** discusses the issues and considers what constitutes a successful policy and how a school can measure it.

Finally, **Warwick Dyer** discusses the importance of clear roles and responsibilities in the management of difficult pupils.

A model – the R A F I E process:

This is a 5 Stage problem-solving model which informs much of the work of the Tower Hamlets Support for Learning Service teachers both at individual and institutional levels. This was the model used by the team in their work with schools.

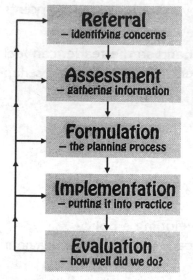

Referral – identifying concerns
: This is your first point of reference - concerns / issues / objectives are identified and agreed.

Assessment – gathering information
: Gathering and examining information through existing documents / practice / policy / systems - to determine agreed baselines and to inform analysis.

Formulation – the planning process
: Analysis of assessment results / data to determine what needs to happen for agreed change to take place - Define targets and success criteria.

Implementation – putting it into practice
: Implementation of agreed strategies designed to bring about desired changes including arrangements for monitoring.

Evaluation – how well did we do?
: Measuring change in relation to agreed targets - determine and agree what needs to happen next. Also, what positive and negative outcomes have there been which weren't planned?

This model describes how the whole policy development process can take place. It indicates the steps that need to be followed. It is not necessarily a linear process, but can respond to feedback and changes that occur throughout the process of the project. A clear **evaluation** may lead back into any of the other stages. It may indicate that further **assessment** is needed, that **reformulation** is necessary or that changes need to be made to the **intervention.** The diagram is intended to indicate that this cyclical process may take place at any stage of the project. The model may apply just as much to individual elements of the project as to the whole thing.

Two other points are worth noting:

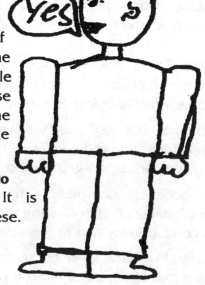

- **That change does not just occur at the end of a project.** The very process itself encourages change. For instance, the assessment process, which involves people reflecting on their practice, will in itself cause change and development through the identification of issues and the making visible of practice and opinions.

- **That there may be unintended outcomes to a project,** both positive or negative. It is important to recognise and acknowledge these.

This book has mostly developed from the work undertaken in a number of schools in the London Borough of Tower Hamlets over the past two years. The work with schools was made possible by joint LEA and DfEE GEST funding for 'Disaffected Pupils'. Throughout the work, we have referred schools to the excellent contents of the DfEE circulars which have come to be known as the *'Six Pack'*, the official title being *'Pupils with Problems'* (Circulars 8 – 13/94).

We would like to recommend that schools embarking on whole school policy work in the area of behaviour should consult in particular DfEE Circular 8/94 *'Pupil Behaviour and Discipline'* and the 'companion' Circular 9/94 *'The Education of Children with Emotional and Behavioural Difficulties'*. These circulars are full of clear and 'common-sensical' definitions and guidelines which schools should take in to consideration when planning whole school approaches to discipline and behaviour. Circular 9/94 *'The Education of Children with Emotional and Behavioural Difficulties'* provides sound practical support to the implementation of the SEN Code of Practice for pupils with emotional and behavioural difficulties and shows how the SEN Policy and the Behaviour and Discipline Policy are linked. Its definitions of emotional and behavioural difficulties are some of the most accessible we have come across.

A sound knowledge of the contents of these circulars would be an excellent basis for a school's preparation for inspection. All the advice, strategies and materials we have presented in this volume correspond closely to what is considered to be good practice by the DfEE in relation to the management of behaviour in schools. We hope that the way in which we have interpreted the circulars through the approaches outlined in this book will support any school, in particular those that may be motivated to read this by reason of a forthcoming inspection.

Schools will inevitably go about the process of policy development in their own way. This is to be encouraged, just in the way that no two schools will develop the same policy. Some schools will feel at home with a very precise and organised structure such as the one presented by Alastair Ross in Chapter 6. Others will feel more at home with a more organic approach or may feel that they have substantial portions of a policy in existence and merely want to consolidate certain aspects.

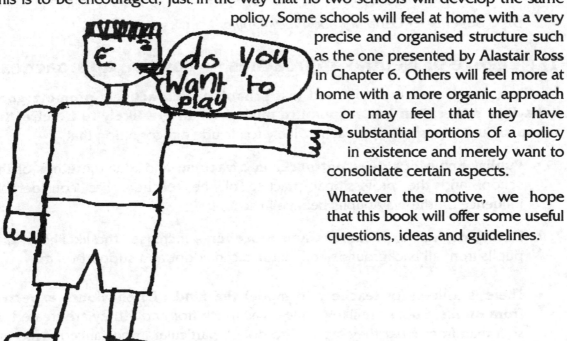

Whatever the motive, we hope that this book will offer some useful questions, ideas and guidelines.

1. WHY HAVE A BEHAVIOUR POLICY?

'Schools can and do make a difference...'

Schools are places of learning and it is important that behaviour is managed so that the aims of the school can be achieved. **The purpose of a behaviour policy is to support this process** through:

- *The creation of a positive and orderly atmosphere where teaching and learning can take place*

- *The creation of a safe environment for pupils and staff through the clarification of expectations, roles, rights and responsibilities*

- *The reduction of teacher stress through the identification of effective systems and practices*

- *Addressing the demands of changing conditions and approaches*

CHANGING CONDITIONS AND APPROACHES

This section outlines key issues which schools should bear in mind when developing a behaviour policy:

1) *Negative or Neutral approaches* → *Positive approaches*
2) *Individual discipline* → *Collegial approach*
3) *Control* → *Cooperation*
4) *Behaviour management as a personal issue* → *A 'procedural' approach*
5) *Severity* → *Certainty and Predictability*

1) Negative or Neutral approaches → Positive approaches

It is increasingly widely recognised that **schools which actively promote good behaviour rather than just respond to misbehaviour are likely to be effective schools**. Such a positive approach is likely to include a recognition that:

- **Pupils' behaviour does not occur in a vacuum** and that the ethos of the school and the professional practice of the teachers has considerable influence on the way pupils behave in school.

- **Having explicit expectations and procedures** increases the likelihood that pupils from all backgrounds and cultures can adopt and support them.

- There is a need for **teachers to model the kind of behaviours expected from pupils.** Pupils are likely to learn as much from *how* they are treated by staff than from *what* they are told to do. Of particular importance maybe the way conflicts and disagreements are sorted out.

- It is important to **engage the commitment of all members of the school community** – pupils, teaching staff and non-teaching staff, parents and governors, so that all groups see the policy as being beneficial to them. An approach which recognises that everybody has both rights *and* responsibilities is likely to achieve this.

- **Effective acknowledgement of appropriate behaviour needs to be planned** rather than left to chance. This recognises that **it is much easier to give attention for inappropriate behaviour** than for appropriate behaviour. Even when appropriate behaviour / improvements are recognised, the amount of teacher attention given to this is frequently much less than for misbehaviour.

- **Being in a school, the learning process itself and growing up are not necessarily easy or comfortable processes** and that the school can address these issues in different ways. The school needs to have ways of addressing the 'affective curriculum' – of acknowledging that pupils have feelings. Schools that don't find legitimate opportunities to acknowledge pupils' feelings will find that pupils will demonstrate them anyway – frequently in a disruptive manner!

- **Appropriate behaviour mangement styles can minimise or prevent much difficult behaviour.** This would include sensible routines as well as clear roles and expectations. It should be recognised that behaviour management is no substitute for well-planned and stimulating lessons. Pupils that are stimulated by the work tend not to be disruptive.

- **The management of behaviour can be planned**, in a similar way to the curriculum, particularly with reference to repeated behaviour difficulties. This is particularly important because managing behaviour can be personally stressful as well as challenging at a professional level.

- Pupils self-esteem will be enhanced if they are encouraged to **take responsibility for themselves and their learning.** This would include encouraging pupils to take responsibility at a personal level as well as contributing socially, perhaps through a School's Council

2) Individual discipline → Collegial approach

Over recent years there has been a change of culture in education where discipline was seen very much as an individual's responsibility. This has sometimes meant the use of, or threat of, physical punishment or at least a 'dominating' approach. Such threats are no longer possible and schools are discovering that the strengths of these approaches can be replaced by the effective use of a collegial approach.

These changes therefore include:

- A **closer involvement and teamwork** with colleagues in the teaching situation through team teaching / use of support teachers / development of departments / year groups
- A need for clarity of roles
- A need for a **consistent approach to behaviour** congruent with the values of the school
- A need to link with the **SEN Code of Practice / IEPs**

3) Control → Cooperation

There is increasing recognition that it is not possible to 'make pupils do things'; that it is not appropriate or practicable to attempt to control them. (It is of course important that teachers have control over the teaching situation). **The positive approach is concerned with developing the relationship between pupils such that they see their needs best being met by cooperating with the school.** McGuiness [1993] discusses how in the process of developing a relationship with pupils, it is important to communicate to them in such a way that they feel valued.

There are behaviour management styles which make a cooperative relationship more or less likely. Bill Rogers [1991] discusses a **Decisive / Assertive style** of behaviour management which aims to avoid the pitfalls of an **Aggressive / Dominating style** or an **Unassertive / Indecisive style** (which can trigger-off inappropriate behaviour themselves).

A teacher may have little power as an individual teacher but working with others as a team can set and enforce acceptable limits of behaviour. This view links in with the use of a **progressive** or a **stepped approach** to responding to misbehaviour at the classroom / whole-school level. These elements contribute to a **predictability** which not only enhances pupils' sense of control but also **reduces anxiety and uncertainty**. It means that pupils (and teachers) will feel that they know **where they are** and **what is going to happen next**.

4) Behaviour management as a personal issue → A 'procedural' approach

Schools need to agree behavioural expectations, limits and responses. Many teachers feel that they can only act decisively if they have reached the limit of their personal tolerance of the situation – *I've had enough!* Apart from making it difficult to have a consistent whole school approach, this makes behaviour management a personal issue – *'I'm sanctioning you because you've pushed me too far!'* rather than *'Because you have broken the agreed rule.'* In this way it also encourages the shift of responsibility for the pupil's behaviour back to them – encouraging the view that their behaviour was a matter of *their choice*.

By making responses to behaviour 'procedural' rather than personal, the emotional temperature can be kept down and pupils can find it easier to cooperate with the process itself and 'take it on board.'

A procedural approach to dealing with disruptive behaviour includes:

- *Even* when managing behaviour, where at all possible, **keep the focus on the learning.**

- **Having the possibility of many steps up the ladder of response**. McManus [1993] discusses how schools who refer quickly to senior members of staff also tend to be high excluding schools.

- **Minimising the amount of overt attention** given to dealing with misbehaviour. One method is to use something like the *Incident Sheet* in the examples section of this book which would mean that that pupil has to focus on the behaviour causing concern without necessarily having the teacher's attention.

- **Making sure there is a minimum of pay-off** in terms of, teacher or peer attention / entertaining teacher response / avoidance of work.

5) Severity → Certainty and Predictability

Bill Rogers emphasises that it is the **certainty** of the consequences rather than their **severity** that is often the effective element in responses to misbehaviour. If the pupil knows the teacher will catch up with them sooner or later, the *'See If I Can Get Away With It'* game will seem a less interesting proposition.

If staff can act in consistent, predictable ways which aim to restrict intervention to the minimum necessary, it is more likely to mean:

- A reduction in anxiety (teacher's and pupil's) and other powerful emotions

- There will always be the possibility of a stronger response next time as well as the pupil being more likely to accept the consequence as legitimate – *'it's a fair cop guv!'*

- There will be little 'pay-off' and a minimum of testing-out behaviour.

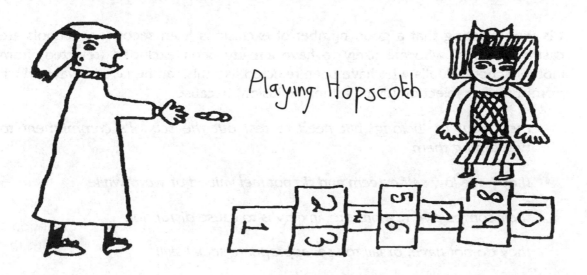

Playing Hopscotch

BELONGING

A. H. Maslow in his hierarchy of human needs indicates the importance of the 'need to belong'. Dreikurs [(1982)] focuses on this within the school situation and identifies two key 'student goals' as **needing to belong** and **needing to have attention**. He discusses how pupils who fail to achieve these goals legitimately can resort to increasingly disruptive behaviours to achieve them. What these views emphasise is the importance of the **relationship** that the pupil is able to achieve with the school. One difficulty that a behaviour policy needs to address is that schools can react to disruptive behaviour (or acts of disaffection) with increasingly controlling methods. Such responses can be experienced by the pupil as increasingly rejecting of *them* not just their behaviour, thus causing a vicious circle.

Certainty and Predictability

Certainty and predictability are more likely to occur if:

1) *Schools have clear rules and consistently reinforced limits.*

2) *There is previous discussion with pupils about fair and related consequences for misbehaviour (and appropriate behaviour).*

3) *Pupils are warned (where possible) before the imposition of a consequence.*

4) *Staff act firmly and confidently, as well as in a respectful manner.*

5) *Staff make consequence as small as possible to allow for stronger responses to be made if necessary. Doing this will also minimise the likelihood of creating resentment.*

6) *Staff follow up incidents if they cannot be dealt with immediately, even if it is some days later.*

7) *Staff make it clear to the pupil that they have been forgiven, but the matter has not been forgotten: that is, if the pupil repeats the behaviour (perhaps within a particular timescale), they will inevitably move another step up the teacher's hierarchy of response.*

It is worth noting that a good number of exclusions from secondary schools are 'casual entrants' who are likely to have already been excluded (rejected) from another school. Pupils who have been rejected like this can behave in ways which prompt further rejection (even further exclusion) because:

> *they want to 'belong' but need to test out the school's commitment to welcoming them*

> *they have low self-esteem and do not feel valued or worthwhile*

> *their compulsive response to anxiety is to cause disruption*

> *they do not have, or fail to use, appropriate social skills*

---

the only way they know how to have some control in the situation is to disrupt

they can gain peer-status or maintain a reputation by behaving badly

they can avoid the pain of further rejection by taking the initiative themselves

they are afraid they cannot live up to the demands or expectations placed on them

they do not feel that the school has anything to offer them

they do not feel that their concerns matter to the school

they need a focus for their feelings of anger and resentment

they feel a failure and can blame the school for letting them down

Some schools plan a programme of induction in order to attempt to forestall or minimise these difficulties and try to take the initiaitive in the development of a positive relationship with the pupil. It will require a clear and positive effort on the part of the school as even a neutral response is likely to be experienced by the pupil as rejection. Understandably, schools can experience an ambivalence towards such pupils which can undermine the likelihood of success. **An effective programme of induction** could include strategies such as:

A gradual adoption of a full timetable

A careful process of monitoring and empathic support

Setting up a 'Storm Home' arrangement (described below)

Positive involvement of the pupil's peers

This might be a 'pupil buddy system' or a process similar to Anatol Pikas' 'shared concern' method.

One primary school uses the 'Induction Booklet' shown in the Chapter 11

Developing peer support in the induction process

This takes the form of asking the class (or appropriate group of pupils) to identify what it must be like for the new pupil then asking how they can be involved in improving the situation:

What must it be like for .... coming here?

What might make it difficult for them to fit in?

How do you think they might feel?

Then...

Is there anything we could do to improve the situation for them?

Don Clarke

Storm Home

One strategy used in some schools for helping manage children who have serious difficulties in behaving is called Storm Home. A member of staff (not necessarily a teacher) volunteers if they feel that they have a fairly positive relationship with the pupil in question. There is usually at least one member of staff that actually quite likes even the most difficult of pupils (especially if they don't actually have to teach them on a regular basis). This person, or persons, (the more the merrier for the most extreme pupils) then makes themselves available for the pupil, if a) the class teacher suspects things are becoming or likely to become too much for the pupil, or b) if the pupil themselves thinks that a break from the class would be helpful. It is helpful if this member of staff is not a senior member of staff so that they are unlikely to be involved in disciplining the pupil. This then allows for the staff member to act supportively towards the pupil in times of crisis; for the child this can offset the feeling that 'the whole school is against them'.

The author has taken the name Storm Home from a story by Garrison Keillor which beautifully illustrates the importance for some children to know that there is a safe place for them to go when things get rough. For those children, just knowing that a 'storm home' exists can make some storms bearable, when otherwise they perhaps wouldn't have been.

WHY MANAGING DIFFICULT BEHAVIOUR IS DIFFICULT
Pupils have feelings...

Pupils who feel good about themselves, find the work satisfying, have positive relationships with peers and staff – do not tend to be a cause for concern. Feelings may not necessarily be the *cause* of pupils' misbehaviour but they certainly play a significant part in the process of disruption.

Pupils who feel bored:
> *will find more entertaining activities to engage in*

Pupils who feel stupid:
> *will behave in ways which avoid them having to face those feelings*

Pupils who do not feel as if they 'belong' to the institution:
> *will also feel that they have little to lose by disrupting it*

Pupils who do not feel safe:
> *will find ways to behave which will create familiar and predictable patterns of behaviour in those around them*

Repetitive misbehaviour is usually the result of unresolved distressing experiences which have been triggered-off by some aspect of the current situation. Because of the unresolved emotional element in a distress experience, the child has not been able to assimilate and make sense of the experience. It seems that children have a natural tendency to try to engage other people's help in resolving these painful feelings and trying to make sense of the situations from which they arose.

A very basic example would be a child who has been frightened, running for its mother for safety and then bursting into tears. Teachers need to use behaviour management styles that minimise those kinds of feelings when they do occur and, if possible, avoid triggering them off in the first place. Some behaviour management styles actually add to the distress that a pupil might be experiencing, thus making the matter worse and also making further repetitions of the difficult behaviour more likely. Calmness, firmness, fairness and predictability are qualities which are likely to minimise difficulties.

Teachers have feelings too...

It seems clear that the management of behaviour problems is qualitatively different from other kinds of problems that occur in schools. Behaviour problems have the power to generate very powerful feelings in staff. As professionals, staff often have to manage such feelings whilst trying to carry out their teaching duties 'normally'. No wonder this aspect of teaching can contribute significantly to the levels of stress.

Managing difficult behaviour can feel extremely difficult because it can challenge teachers both professionally and personally in a very powerful way. It should also be noted that it is not necessarily the most disruptive behaviour that can be the most difficult to manage. At a personal level, it is the behaviour which connects with teachers' own 'baggage'; at a professional level it is often the 'low level, high frequency behaviours' identified by the Elton Report [1989]. A key purpose of a behaviour policy is to provide a structure to maximise the possibilities of creating a learning and teaching environment that is secure, predictable and fair – for pupils and for staff. The aim of a policy is to make clear what is expected from all parties – a clarification of roles and responsibilities of all in the school community. This is most effectively established by consultation and involvement of all members of the school community.

'Schools can and do make a difference...'

Teachers cannot control what backgrounds the pupils come from or dictate what life experiences they have. However, they can have some control over how much those elements intrude into the day to day life of the school. It can be difficult for a pupil whose life is filled with powerful feelings from events in their home life, to put them aside and attend to the educational demands placed upon them in school. This is particularly so if the structures, processes and relationships within the school remind them of the other difficulties in their lives. A behaviour policy and its associated practices should be aimed at creating and supporting those structures, processes and relationships which:

- *emphasise predictability and fairness*
- *raise rather than diminish pupils' self-esteem*
- *encourage self-discipline and self-responsibility*

2. WHAT A BEHAVIOUR POLICY SHOULD CONTAIN

'Minds like parachutes, only function when open'

A behaviour policy should contain the following elements:

- The general aims of the school
- A description of the rights and responsibilities of all members of the school community
- Rules / Code of Conduct
- A description of the ways in which the school encourages good behaviour
- A description of unacceptable behaviours
- What the school does when pupils do misbehave
- Links to other policies eg SEN / Equal Opportunities / Anti-bullying / Anti-racism
- Areas of special concern

A number of schools have found it useful if there are at least two documents:

The Policy Statement which covers all the relevant issues aimed at pupils and parents

A Handbook which sets out in detail:

- the responsibilities of different staff

- agreed procedures and practice for encouraging appropriate behaviour

- descriptions of different levels of misbehaviour

- the agreed range of responses, consequences and sanctions related to different levels of misbehaviour as well as in particular circumstances such as behaviour on trips

Some schools have also found it helpful to encourage playground staff to develop a handbook for their own use.

The General Aims of the School

The purpose of a behaviour policy is to support the educational and other aims of the school and to ensure that the conduct of all members of the school community is consistent with the values of the school.

Rights and Responsibilities

These rights will be based upon the values held by the school. The values identified by schools often include:

Mutual respect   Respect for property
Fairness and Honesty   Care and consideration of others
Self-respect   Self-discipline

The rights implicit in such values would include:

The right to be safe   The right to fair treatment
The right to be heard   The right to be treated with respect
The right to be able to learn and teach without unnecessary interruption

Rights do not exist in a vacuum. They can only happen if others take responsibility for protecting those rights. They are the other side of the coin.

Responsibilities of pupils might include:

Letting other pupils get on with their work
Sorting out disagreements without fighting

Responsibilities of teachers might include:

Providing appropriate work
Treating all pupils with respect and fairness

The school can identify the rights and responsibilities of different groups within the school community through a process of consultation and discussion.

Rules / Code of Conduct

The 'school rules' or 'class rules' or Code of Conduct are a summary of the responsibilities of pupils. Some behaviour policies contain 'rules' of how other people are expected to behave, including staff, parents and visitors. This reinforces the idea that behaviour is not just a childish issue but one which relates to everybody – *we all benefit when we all behave well*.

Rules are effective when they are:

- *Few, reasonable and fair*

- *Explained, discussed with and taught to pupils*

- *Simple and precise*

- *Enforced and enforceable*

- *Positive – describe the behaviour the school wants to see*

Rules should cover:

- *Noise*

- *How pupils get teacher's attention*

- *The way people treat one another*

- *Resolving difficulties and conflicts*

- *Movement and safety*

Pupils can be encouraged to take ownership of the rules if they are involved in the process of their development. Examples of this can be found in the materials at the end of the book. This can take place through a guided discussion of rights and responsibilities. Pupils will often see things in negative terms and should be encouraged to redefine them positively – 'We will all walk around the classroom' rather than 'No running'. Where possible, use their choice of wording. Rules do not have to be static but can respond to the current concerns of the class – or class teacher. The written rules may be rather bland, but they can be filled out either in writing or verbally with 'what this rule means is...' If a list of rules is visible, they can be a constant reminder as well as being able to be referred to non-verbally. Misbehaviour can be interrupted with the question, 'Which rule are you breaking?' requiring the pupil to think and respond rather than just stop misbehaving – thus encouraging self-discipline.

It can create greater consistency if **the rules (and consequences) belong to the class** and so are adopted by different staff that may take them. This can be of particular benefit to new or temporary staff.

One school had on the cover of their behaviour policy – 'Happiness is knowing the rules'. This does not seem entirely likely, but certainly, knowing the rules can reduce anxiety and all that that can lead to.

'What the school does to prevent misbehaviour and encourage appropriate behaviour' – The positive policy

> 'Schools can and do make a difference. They have the capacity to lead, support and encourage pupils in developing good behaviour and in learning to play a responsible role both within school and in the wider world.' (Elton Report)

A behaviour policy needs to emphasise that the school does not 'just expect pupils to behave well', but that it has a responsibility to organise itself in such a way that it positively encourages the desired behaviours. Schools that 'do make a difference' tend to be those which, whilst managing pupils' behaviour, do so in ways that keep pupils' 'minds open' and in consequence learn from their experience.

A behaviour policy will do this through:

Defining the behaviours desired and making expectations clear

Using effective and stimulating teaching methods

Staff modelling appropriate behaviour

Actively teaching strategies for resolving difficulties

Providing appropriate opportunities for pupils to have control over their learning and environment

Ensuring good behaviour and efforts are acknowledged systematically

Minimising attention given to bad behaviour

Developing the 'affective' curriculum through, for example 'circle work' – pupils being able to talk about themselves, their concerns and their feelings

Creating a safe and predictable environment

Communicating to all pupils that they are valued, whatever their background or abilities

Teaching the social skills required to participate fully in the school

Dreikurs[1982], Rogers[1990] and others use the term **Logical Consequences** to describe a school's response to poor behaviour. Three aims of Logical Consequences are:

- *To encourage pupils to understand that their actions have a logical effect in the world*

- *To encourage an awareness of personal choices and responsibility for one's actions – to become self-disciplined*

- *To try to maintain or build a positive working relationship*

In practice, the difference between 'Logical Consequences' / punishments / sanctions may be only a matter of viewpoint, but nevertheless can make considerable differences in terms of the quality of the relationships and the ethos generated.

Negative attention / positive attention

Some pupils learn that they can reliably gain a teacher's attention and peer attention by misbehaving. Their experience also tells them that being well behaved or trying hard rarely provides them with the reliability, frequency or the quantity of attention that they crave. For teachers', their responses to misbehaviour can sometimes make them 'feel better' by venting some of their irritation which in the long-term only make further misbehaviour more likely.

In the process of developing a policy a school needs to consider the implicit lessons they are teaching their pupils with regard to gaining attention.

Behaviour policies often include well worked out systems and procedures for responding to disruptive behaviour, such as:

> *being 'looked at' / noticed*
> *being told off, sometimes right across a classroom*
> *being lectured at*
> *having the class' attention directed towards them*
> *being sent to see high status staff*

Plenty of attention! Important questions for schools to ask are:

> *How can we minimise the amount of attention we give to pupils when they are being attention-seeking or disruptive?*

> *Are we providing enough ways to achieve appropriate attention through having efforts and successes acknowledged? Are these means reliable? Do all pupils have the necessary skills?*

Pupils gain a sense of themselves from the way people around them respond to them. Pupils do need their efforts and successes acknowledged and valued (not necessarily rewarded!) Praise or positive feedback when it does come, is often verbal and its effects can quickly evaporate – particularly for those whom success is not a familiar occurrence.

So other important questions schools can ask are:

How can we make our praise and positive feedback visible or tangible?

Are we systematic? Or do we only do things when we remember or feel like it?

A visible or tangible symbol of the pupil's achievement:

- *Can 'radiate' teacher attention long after the event and when feelings of self-doubt and discouragement might otherwise have made them forget*

- *Can be referred to when things are not going quite so well*

- *Can be shown to friends and parents and prompt further appropriate praise and attention*

- *Can be as quick as a 'Smiley Face' or a 'Well Tried' written on some work*

- *Can be as grand as having all the whole school clap you in assembly*

A description of unacceptable behaviours

A policy would contain a description of the range of behaviours the school defined as being inconsistent with the rules. It would indicate that the school recognised that some behaviours were trivial (but never the less undesirable) and that other behaviours were moderately serious as well as other instances of misbehaviour as being very serious. It would also emphasise that repeated misbehaviour would be treated as significantly more seriously than one-off instances.

What the school does when pupils do misbehave

The policy would indicate the range of unacceptable behaviour. The handbook for staff would record the behaviours that give concern in the school, from trivial through to extremely serious. Staff need to arrive at a working consensus on the seriousness of different types of behaviour. Agreement also needs to be reached on an equivalent list of consequences or sanctions. The table on the page opposite gives examples drawn from a discussion in a school. This process needs to be gone through in order that pupils experience the behaviour management as fair as well as the staff feeling confident in the range of options available to them as behaviour (perhaps) becomes increasingly serious. Attention must be given to how repeated misbehaviour is to be treated more seriously and also how this range of response is communicated to pupils.

Schools have found it helpful to define the seriousness of behaviours by answering the following questions:

What behaviours do you think can be effectively managed within the normal level of classroom management?

What behaviours do you think will require the use of consequences or sanctions?

What behaviours do you think will require the the involvement of senior members of staff?

It is important to discuss responses to both one-off and repeated occurrences.

A Hierarchy of Seriousness

The following are three broad categories of behaviour difficulties:

Level 1 or 'Trivial' behaviours:

Those are behaviours which will be dealt with by the class or subject teacher through the use of minimal interactions aimed at refocussing the pupil back on task. Bill Rogers discusses a repertoire of strategies that teachers frequently use which he refers to as Least Intrusive to Most Intrusive strategies. He places great emphasis on keeping the level of the interaction to a minimum and for the teacher to always be aware of their next step, should it be necessary. These would include: diversions, rule reminders, positive directions, use of positioning in the classroom and closeness to the pupil

Behaviour in this school – 3 levels of seriousness		
LEVEL 1	**LEVEL 2**	**LEVEL 3**
Teasing		
Pushing in		
Interrupting teacher		
Attention seeking / Clowning around		
Spoiling other pupils' games		
Telling tales		
Avoiding work / wasting time		
Eating in class		
Being noisy		
Name calling		
Running inside		
Spitting		
Arguing about everything	Arguing back	
Hindering other children	Hindering other children	
Cheekiness	Rudeness	
Cussing	Cussing	
	Rudeness to staff	
	Lying	
	Biting	
	Graffiti	Vandalism
	Hitting back (parents' orders)	Hitting back (parents' orders)
	Kicking	Vicious Kicking
Play-fighting / horseplay	Fighting / squabbles	Fighting / Thuggery
Uncooperativeness	Refusal to follow instructions	Dangerous refusal to follow instructions
Using swear words	Swearing at pupils	Swearing at staff
		Lying
		Racial Abuse
		Stealing
		Physical abuse of staff
		Verbal abuse of staff
		Extortion
		Running out of school
		Bullying

Gathering staff perceptions of behaviour in the school

A list produced from a staff group who discussed the seriousness of behaviours that they were concerned about. Some behaviours (such as attention seeking) are 'fuzzy' and would need clarification. Gaining consensus on the degrees of seriousness of certain behaviours such as different kinds of swearing and fighting which can sometimes be trivial and other times be very serious, can take some time!

Level 2 or Moderately Serious behaviours:

These behaviours would probably require:

- *A clear reminder of the rules or limits*
- *A reminder of the consequence of repeating the behaviour*
- *Applying the consequence which can either be immediate – 'I want you to move to the empty seat over there now' – or deferred – 'You will have to finish your work at breaktime'*

This level of misbehaviour includes **moderately serious misbehaviour** or **repeated minor misbehaviour**. It would be expected that such behaviours would be dealt with by the class/ subject teacher.

Level 3 or Very Serious behaviours:

This level of misbehaviour would require the involvement of more senior colleagues. Such involvement would probably take place outside lesson times. Ideally, the involvement of senior staff would be 'stepped' so that a sense of forward momentum can be maintained. The section on the opposite page contains a primary example which could easily be adapted for secondary school use. Important issues to consider in the development of consistency of approach across classes are:

- *What kinds and levels of behaviour warrant the involvement of senior colleagues?*

- *How colleagues will become involved – referral systems etc?*

- *When involving a more senior colleague agreeing:*
  - *what they are expected to do*
  - *how the referring teacher continues to be involved so that they are seen to be making things more serious rather than passing on the responsibility*

- *How things may be taken further:*
  - *pupil report and behaviour monitoring procedures*
  - *involvement of Head Teacher / Parents / Governors*
  - *exclusions*
  - *links with SEN stages 1 – 5*

- *The nature of the recording and monitoring process*

A pupil should be able to gauge how serious things are by what happens to them. They should also be clear about the next step in the process and what they would have to do to get them there. This last point reinforces the pupil's ownership of their own behaviour.

Removal-from-classroom procedure

Level 3 behaviour should not be confused with the occasional need to have a pupil temporarily removed from a classroom. Although a senior member of staff might be the person operating the Time Out facility, the follow-up would be carried out by the subject teacher.

What a behaviour policy should contain

When the Head Teacher becomes involved

The following series of levels is a way of cueing to the pupil and their parents the increasing seriousness of their behaviour. It also provides a good deal of flexibility so that mitigating circumstances can be taken into consideration when necessary.

HT Level 1
HT investigates the situation and notes it down formally in Head Teacher's Log. Passes back to class teacher who applies sanction and writes informal letter telling the parents of the situation and inviting them to contact the class teacher if they want.

HT Level 2
As for Level 1 but class teacher writes formal letter requesting the parents to make contact to discuss the matter.

HT Level 3
As for Level 2 but pupil put on class teacher's report for feedback to HT and Parent. Warning of official involvement of HT for next incident.

HT Level 4
HT becomes directly involved and sends a formal letter informing the parent of the situation and inviting them to contact them if they want. Copy to class teacher.

HT Level 5
Applies sanction and sends a formal letter informing the parent of the situation and requesting that they contact the HT to discuss the matter. Copy to class teacher. Warning of report next time.

HT Level 6
HT applies sanction and sends a formal letter informing the parent of the situation and requesting that they contact the HT to discuss the matter. Pupil put on HT report. Discussion with class teacher about in-class strategies. Warning of possible exclusion.

HT Level 7
Possible exclusion

If a member of staff believes that a child's behaviour warrants the involvement of HT or DHT they communicate this to them in writing. If the HT then agrees that the matter does warrant their official involvement then the above series of steps is a possible hierarchy of response (which can be entered at any point depending upon severity and context).

The key issue here is that there is a range of increasingly serious responses to persistent misbehaviour **even once the head teacher has become involved**. In the initial stages the headteacher is involved but the class teacher still remains 'in charge'. This progressively changes through the levels. The aim is to balance flexibility for the staff with consistency and forward momentum for the pupil. If the frequency or seriousness of further misbehaviour is reduced, it is possible to drop back to a lower level.

Special areas of concern

The policy should also indicate special areas of concern such as racism, sexual harassment or bullying. It should also show how the behaviour policy links in with other policies including Anti-Bullying, Equal Opportunities and SEN.

Links with SEN

It should be recognised that repeated misbehaviour can:

Constitute a Special Educational Need in itself

Be indicative of a learning difficulty

Be indicative of lack of appropriate social skills

Be indicative of emotional upset related to in-school circumstances eg bullying

Be indicative of emotional upset related to out-of-school circumstances eg abuse / bereavement / family turmoil / anxiety or depression

Concerns relating to repeated misbehaviour will warrant a child being placed on the SEN register.

Therefore, class teachers need to review a child's progress and achievement in the light of this. Some of the following questions might be useful:

Could the misbehaviour be a strategy to avoid work? If so, could this be because the child feels:

- *That they don't understand what is required of them*
- *That they don't have the appropriate experience or knowledge*
- *That they are likely to fail in some way (in their own eyes / parents' eyes / teachers' eyes)*
- *That they feel overwhelmed or confused by the work*
- *That it will create difficulties with peers*
- *That it will set up expectations about them which they feel anxious about being able to sustain*
- *Too anxious or unhappy about other things to focus on the work*

Might the subject matter of the work contain intentional or unintentional painful reminders of unpleasant situations in their home lives?

Are there particular contexts when the child misbehaves or attempts to avoid work?

- *Particular subjects or topics?*
- *New / Written / Practical / Individual / Creative / work?*
- *Physical activities?*
- *Particular working groups or partners?*
- *When I present work verbally and without visual cues*
- *When I give several instructions at once without writing them up on the board*
- *When I don't make it clear what is expected of them – I don't show them examples*

Criteria for inclusion in SEN register

Staff will need to discuss the following questions:

- *What behavioural criteria do class / subject teachers use to determine whether a child is causing enough concern to have them entered on the SEN register?*
- *Is there consistency between teachers?*
- *What behavioural criteria does the SENCO use for moving pupils onto stages 1 – 3?*

Objective criteria would include:

The **nature** of the behaviour

> *A description of what the pupil might be seen doing*

The **severity** of the behaviour

> *Fighting, for instance might be – a minor scuffle resulting from a mutual disagreement – to a vicious and unprovoked attack*
>
> *Swearing might range from the use of a particular range of words in conversation or as a result of making a mistake to a direct verbal attack on a member of staff.*

The **frequency** of the behaviour

> *Calling out several times during a lesson*
>
> *Being cheeky to ancillary staff several times over a number of days*
>
> *Getting into minor scuffles over a period of weeks*

The **duration** of the behaviour

> *Tapping a pencil continuously*
>
> *Conversing endlessly with peers*

The **generality** of the behaviour

> *If the behaviour occurs across a number of contexts / subject areas*

Staff should discuss these areas and agree on the degree of seriousness of behaviour and also appropriate levels of response.

Policies take time to develop and can grow and adapt as circumstances change. As with all aspects of school life, there is not usually the resources to achieve everything immediately and so it can be useful for a school to have a behaviour policy development plan.

Playing nicely

---

3.   PLANNING FOR CHANGE

Travellers who have not clearly identified their destination, will find it difficult to plan a route, or recognize signposts along the way. They may well arrive at a good place and pass on through, without ever knowing that it was where they wanted to be. Or, they may go in totally the wrong direction and end up some place which was worse than where they started.

The way schools plan for change is through their Management / Development Plan. The school's vision for future development and the process of change should provide the starting point for all discussion about policy and practice. Having a Management Plan helps to ensure that every member of the organisation is moving toward the same goals, and feels part of common purpose. The process of whole school policy development mirrors the process of development for the Management Plan, and of necessity involves all sections of the school community.

The development of a whole school behaviour policy should be a process involving all sections of the school community. The DFE states:

'Although the Governing Body should take a clear lead in proposing principles and standards, the school's behaviour policy should be worked out in a spirit of co-operation with the Head Teacher and the whole of the teaching and non-teaching staff. The policy should be discussed with parents and pupils and should feature in the annual report to parents...' (Circular 8/94, par 19)

While this statement formally identifies the key member groups in the school community, it offers no help with how to effectively involve them all in the process nor what form the process should take. Implicit in the circular's recommendations is the assumption that any behaviour and discipline policy will only be effective if it has the support of the parents and pupils. Furthermore, this support is more likely to be actual rather than notional, if both groups have been involved in the development and implementation process.

How the policy development process is planned and introduced will help to establish the climate. Not all members of the school community have the same status or life experiences. How the process addresses equality of opportunity to participate and encourage individual and all staff groups to make their contribution, will in a large part determine how successful the outcome will be. Therefore it will be important to:

- Make it clear that all contributions will be valued and taken into account.

- Establish a working party to act as a steering committee for the process.

- Ensure that the membership is inclusive and makes provision for all voices to be represented.

Consultation as a process is only meaningful if there is a genuine opportunity for the 'consulted' to feed back into the development process. The time necessary for consultation is more usefully built in alongside the stages of the development process. This allows for differences of view and areas of potential conflict to be addressed along the way. See Chapter 4 – Involving the Whole School Community.

Managing Change

The challenge for any school is how to develop and implement a living and effective behaviour policy, and at the same time, engender a spirit of collaboration throughout the school to support the policy process. Change can be described simply as 'what happens when there is a sufficient desire to move from a point which is not satisfactory to one which will be'.

This simple statement can raise several questions all of which must be either clearly answered or clearly recognised to be unanswerable at the time of embarking on the change.

What Change?

- What do those who desire the change think is unsatisfactory at present?
- Who desires the change (i.e. who thinks the present situation is unsatisfactory)?
- Who might not desire the change?
- What would those who desire the change like to see happen as a result?

What Constrains And What Facilitates The Change?

- What will happen if those desiring the change are either in the minority or in personal or professional positions which do not allow them to lead or manage change?
- How will those who desire the change convince or motivate those who might not desire it?
- What is the minimum requirement for the change to be successful in terms of the different people involved (i.e. what could there be consensus around)?

Will The Change Be Successful?

- YES - if the facilitating and constraining factors balance out positively in favour of the change. This means answering the above questions very carefully
- NO - if the facilitating and constraining factors balance out negatively. This might happen if the questions above have highlighted other more urgent issues which need to be addressed first

Success Criteria

- What will tell you that you have achieved the change? What will you actually see and / or be able to measure?

Unless the questions are addressed and a consensus is reached beforehand between all those who will be affected, the change is unlikely to be effective, workable or lasting. Consensus is seldom easy to achieve, and in some schools attempts to do so will throw up quite profound differences amongst various individuals and groups. However painful a process, such differences are 'better out than in'. These differences need to be acknowledged and then the school needs to move on and establish consensus around the areas on which everyone can agree to act.

Getting Started

In the school projects from which much of the material in this book was drawn, the development of whole school policy was led by a working party of staff. In many cases, parents, governors, mid-day meal supervisors, secretaries, educational psychologists, school nurses, educational social workers, might also have been members of the working party.

In this initial stage of the work schools must attempt to establish consensus around the following questions:

- Why are we developing school policy on behaviour?

- What do we hope to achieve?

- What do we hope will be different in our school, once a new policy has been established?

- What do we hope will be the same?

- How will we know if we have been successful?

- What kinds of information will be needed to monitor and evaluate our progress?

What follows is an outline of the steps which can be taken to help the process get started. By identifying the key concerns of various groups within the school, consensus can be established around:

- Aims

- Objectives

- Success indicators

Swearing at each other

Establishing Consensus - A development activity

A very useful technique for establishing consensus is to pose a series of questions similar to those on the previous pages or those below. These questions explore various aspects around behaviour. As well as attempting to answer these questions this activity will highlight current issues and concerns around behaviour.

First of all, participants are asked to work individually and silently, considering and writing a response to each question. They are asked to identify the positive issues as well as the difficulties and concerns which the questions raise for them. Participants are told that all questions need not be answered, and that they are not solving any problems at this stage or considering particular issues in depth.

1. *What steps are taken to establish a shared sense of values around behaviour in your school?*

2. *Do you think that parents and visitors would say that there is a positive atmosphere and that they feel welcome in school?*

3. *Are there support systems available to support the teacher in the classroom in managing difficult behaviour?*

4. *Does the curriculum offered in your lessons match the needs of all your pupils?*

5. *How is pupils' free time organised and supervised? Does that work?*

6. *What systems do we have for praising / acknowledging / rewarding pupils' appropriate behaviour and work?*

7. *How do we give parents positive feedback about their children's work /behaviour? Have we got a system ?*

The individual activity is followed by a progression of activities in pairs, fours, etc. until there is one group. With each regrouping those responses which go forward represent only the areas of agreement within the group. The process can be quite time consuming, and may usefully form part of a professional training day. Individuals will work best around those issues to which they are personally committed. This will generate the material for consensus around the aims of a behaviour policy and for planning the agenda for the work.

Agreeing Aims

Here is an example of the aims formulated by one secondary school who undertook a consensus exercise.

Aims
This policy will:

Help us develop changes in attitude and changes in behaviour

Be workable and acceptable to all

Encourage pupils to take responsibility for their own behaviour

Encourage self control and respect for self and others

Agreeing Objectives

Working from these very general aims, the same school identified specific problems in the way people behaved in the classroom and in the playground, and they agreed objectives in relation to these.

Objectives
In the classroom:

Everyone to complete the work set

Everyone will acknowledge people's achievements

To have positive discussions without interruptions or shouting out

In the playground and around the school building:

Less bullying or fighting

Less name calling or cussing people's families

More friendliness, especially to newcomers and visitors

Everyone to develop a better way of dealing with conflict; people will not be blamed unfairly

Agreeing success indicators

The school further decided that it would evaluate its success in terms of the development of an agreed policy, specific changes in behaviour as set out in its objectives, and in more general changes in the ethos.

Success Indicators

We will know we have been successful if:

> We produce a written policy on behaviour which is agreed by pupils and staff.

> That policy is reflected in our practice.

> There are changes in behaviour and attitude as set out in our objectives.

> These changes result in a more positive ethos in the school reflected in less disaffection, fewer exclusions, improved attendance, improved levels of achievement.

Defining success indicators enables schools to identify the specific kinds of information they will need to collect prior to the implementation of a policy (see Chapter 4 on Assessment), and at various points during implementation in order to evaluate the success of their policy. (See Chapter 8 on Evaluation)

Being unkind

4. STRUCTURES FOR INVOLVING THE SCHOOL COMMUNITY

Introduction

Developing, implementing and reviewing a Behaviour Policy is a process. It is about communication and interaction between people. The more all the people involved in using the Policy are also involved in developing and agreeing it, the more actively and consistently it will be used.

This chapter is about the structuring of this process.

Our purpose is:

- To encourage active involvement in the process of Policy development
- To encourage all who will be affected by the Policy to have a sense of ownership
- To ensure that this extends to the parents and carers in a visible way
- To encourage a sense of security in staff and pupils so that they can work to their full potential
- To ensure that all concerned have space to think about their responsibilities and actions within a predictable framework
- To ensure that this framework is seen and make it likely that it is experienced as developed and agreed by all
- To encourage the cohesive and consistent implementation of the Policy by all adults concerned
- To ensure that the Policy is actively used by all over time – that it is a living part of school life

What We Mean By 'Staff' – An undervalued resource?

By 'staff' we mean *all* staff – all adults working in the school. This involves a number of roles – mealtime supervisors, secretary, teachers, classroom assistants, premises manager. This will need to be explicitly stated in the Policy Document when acknowledging the contributions of the staff.

It would be helpful if it became usual practice in the school to always say 'teachers' or 'teaching staff' whenever this was the meaning intended and to habitually refer to 'staff' at all other times.

With this would come a sense of the value and dignity of all staff members which might prove of great benefit to the school in the long term. In most schools there is a sharp division between teaching and non-teaching staff. **This is in spite of**

the fact that non-teaching staff that are often in charge of pupils at key times such as the lunch period and interact with pupils in important ways at many other times of the day. These interactions form part of the pupil's picture of school and of themselves at school. They carry over into the classroom and the learning process.

In relation to behaviour, pupils are keenly aware of the level of cooperation and agreement between all staff about rules and procedures. A high level of agreement and cooperation, and the sense of predictability that goes with it, allows pupils the feeling of safety and security so necessary to the risk-taking and experimentation of the learning process. The process of changing perceptions will only happen if the headteacher and SMT believe in it's value to the school and to the educational process. Many factors stand in the way. Among these are: great differentials in pay and conditions of employment, differing class, educational and lifestyle backgrounds and a history of custom and practice. These engender strong feelings which must be addressed.

Best results come where there is a commitment from senior management to value and *act on* the contributions and suggestions of all staff. For headteachers and teaching staff this is often felt as a risk. It is important to keep the pace of change slow, measured and practically based. When thinking of suggestions made by staff unaccustomed to their thoughts and practical ideas being actively sought, it can be *worth* taking some risks. The long term gain in enthusiasm and commitment from using ideas put forward, however imperfect they may *seem*, may be worth the risks taken. Failing to take these risks can represent a serious under-use of human resources.

A temptation is sometimes to decide that *we are all the same*, all equal. This is plainly not the case and is not what is being proposed.

> *In changing perceptions of what we mean by 'staff', the art is to recognise, value and maintain the boundaries between the various roles of staff with an eye to maximising the level of cooperation, commitment, contribution and overlap between the roles.*
>
> *It is the job of the senior management team, and particularly the headteacher, to hold this vision in mind.*

An example:

In one school, after a period of both separate and joint meetings of teaching and non-teaching staff and relevant training, a new system of managing playground behaviour and the sending in of children at lunchtime was introduced. A combination of the new system and an increased feeling of status on the part of the lunchtime supervisors meant that the number of pupils sent in at lunchtime there was immediate and full feedback on the steps taken and the outcomes. This in turn increased the sense of being taken seriously on the part of the lunchtime supervisors and helped to maintain the improvement in the long term. The extra work and time was considered a worthwhile investment.

Core Ingredients and Structure

The Policy Development process can be structured around the following areas:

- The Responsibilities of each main group of people: staff, parents and pupils
- Encouraging and acknowledging good behaviour
- What the school does in response to negative behaviour

These areas can be seen as strands of development which are carried forward concurrently, though each informs and complements the others. They are not the sum total of a Behaviour Policy, but establish an agreed framework for how people will act together. Much will need to be added, possibly later as a Staff Behaviour Policy Handbook, detailing agreed categories of behaviour, particular strategies for promoting good behaviour, specific procedures for different areas of the building, etc. (See examples in Chapter 11)

If the core principles and ingredients are seen by everyone to be developed and agreed collectively at the outset, a positive atmosphere and framework is created for the development and implementation of more detailed strategies and procedures. This detailed work can then take place in an Action Plan over a period of time.

The Core section of the Policy, the public document, could then look like this:

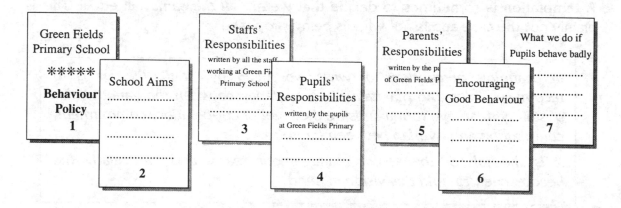

This is one possible way of presenting a Policy. The point is that the structure of the development process needs to match the format of the Core Policy. This will then make sense for all concerned of the development work they put in. For those who come to the school later there is the visible proof of involvement in the statements *'Written by the Pupils (Parents / Staff) of Green Fields Primary'*.

The Responsibilities

A discussion of Responsibilities will necessarily involve considering the Rights of each group and of individuals within the group. If the Responsibilities are defined positively by the groups themselves then the first result is an implicit recognition of the Rights of others, which can then be made explicit at a later stage. The second result is a framework of positively framed codes of conduct covering most of the areas dealt with by the more usual set of rules imposed implicitly or explicitly by the teachers alone.

This approach involves taking a risk. The risk is that each group will define an acceptable and full enough list of Responsibilities. Experience suggests that, if the process is well structured, this invariably happens. Any omissions are usually far outweighed by the gain of everyone feeling that they participated in the process and of having visible proof of this in the written Policy.

It is essential that the written contributions of everyone participating, even if combined together, remain in the words and phrases that they were made in and are not converted into 'school-' or 'teacher-' language. The Responsibilities must have been clearly and visibly written by each group. Referring to them is then far more effective when the Policy is in use. *'This is what you wrote down'*, said to a child, or *'This is what the Parents decided'*, lose their magic when obviously re-written by teachers! The same applies to adults in the school, both teaching and support staff.

Acknowledging Good Behaviour

What we are looking at here is ways in which the school can acknowledge the good behaviour of individuals, classes and possibly year groups. This practice needs to be consistently applied across the school and should be visible to the children and parents. Because the issue is emotive, in many staff groups the idea of rewards and the discussion about acknowledgement can quickly become polarised into whether one should or shouldn't reward. The debate is complex and it may be hard to find a consistent position. Often the result is that individuals or factions among the staff become locked into positions and lose sight of common ground.

If it is accepted among the staff that good behaviour should be recognised and acknowledged in some form, **then the agreed practice needs to be defined and written down,** in a similar way to procedures for dealing with misbehaviour. This activity needs to be undertaken by the staff group as a whole, as it was with defining the Adult's Responsibilities, so that implementation is owned and is consistent across the school. It should be given equal status to defining Sanctions.

The Hierarchy of Sanctions

- **Formulating a framework of response to misbehaviour should be done by the staff working in the school,** without involving the pupils.

- **This hierarchy of responses can be defined *before* fitting these responses**

to particular behaviours. The framework is then there for use and reference by everyone. It is something to turn to and use for negotiation, a secure cornerstone to allay the anxiety of both pupils and staff.

- **The pupils are involved in defining their Responsibilities.** From this they can be involved in defining specific rules, or in looking at what constitutes Minor, Moderately Serious or Very Serious misbehaviour. There is room for negotiation with the pupils, but this is different from who decides what will be done in response to misbehaviour, what the Consequences will be.

For further discussion on a Hierarchy of Sanctions see Chapters 2 and 6.

Principles and Practice of the Development Structure

- **Discussions about the contents of the policy are organised to start small;** they are personal, broken up into manageable segments and move quickly to something written. Whole staff discussions follow when a draft of the section under discussion has been assembled from these written contributions.

- **All written contributions are given status and value.** These contributions are typed, displayed in a central folder and remain in the words and phrases used by those who wrote them.

- **These discussions preferably take place across the usual professional boundaries between teaching and non-teaching staff.** Behaviour affects and is dealt with by staff in all their varying roles. To enhance the status of all sections of the staff group by involving them in formulating the Behaviour Policy can improve the effectiveness of the school's response to misbehaviour.

- **Development and implementation are seen as inter-dependent.** The development work is seen as part of the implementation process and the implementation is structured to arise naturally out of the development process. There is an example of this in the section on Pupils' Responsibilities in the chapter on Developing a Primary Policy.

- **All adults in the school should know what is happening, when and why.** A clear plan for the work, with target dates, is agreed at the outset and displayed. A presentation to all staff at the outset and a central folder displaying all contributions and information gathered can help in this.

- **One person oversees the mechanics of the process, though not the content.** A consultant is entrusted with maintaining the structure of the work and keeping the process to the agreed timetable.

- **Staff agree to act together.** The development timetable will demand that at certain points decisions and agreements must be made. It should be explicitly agreed at the outset that, at these times, all views having been heard and considered, the members of the group have to suspend disagreements and act on the majority view. This involves suspending one's personal monopoly on the truth about what is best to do. **Actually voicing and referring to the need for everyone to act together in this way can give the staff group a feeling of safety and make it easier to contain disagreements.**

How To Do It - General Structure

The process that has been outlined in this chapter is concerned with the involvement of the various groups and roles in the school in the long-term development and implementation of a Behaviour Policy. I have emphasised the importance of structuring this process.

The Governors

In the DFE Circulars *'Pupils With Problems'* (1994) it states that the governors, in consultation with the headteacher and others, **should take the lead in developing the school's overall policy on behaviour.** The governors are asked to lay down general principles in writing. It is then up to the governing body to decide what level of involvement they will have in the development process.

The governors might also choose to **appoint a small committee** to gather and document what they consider to be the school's **strengths** in managing behaviour and to list their **concerns**. This group, in their capacity of giving guidance to the headteacher and staff, could also be charged with responding to sections of the draft Policy as it is written. They might also be involved in deciding on the overall timespan of the work and could reinforce the consultant's task of keeping it to timetable.

These aspects of organisation will vary from school to school. It can be desirable for governor **representation** to be a part of the structure of Behaviour Policy development. Useful ways of doing this are: membership of the **Working Party** as discussed and: attendance of governor representatives at the key **staff meetings** where they can take part in the structured discussions involving pairs with different roles within the school. They are then in a position to understand and report back the flavour of the discussions and approaches being adopted. One other possibility is that governor representatives attend associated **staff training.** All these approaches have been used in schools.

The Facilitator and External Consultants

One person needs to be entrusted with overseeing the mechanics of the process, maintaining the structure of the work, and keeping it to the agreed timetable. Behaviour, as an issue, is wide-ranging and can be emotive. **A flexible but firm facilitator can help the group remain both on task and purposeful.**

The facilitator needs to:

- have the full backing and trust of headteacher
- be acceptable to staff
- be seen as independent-minded and fair
- have full access to school decision-making process, possibly as a member of the SMT

Behaviour is central to the school process - to learning and teaching and to communication between pupils and between staff. It can divide and unite very powerfully. It can become a focus for misunderstandings, divisions and dissatisfactions.

It is often the focal point for lack of communication, stirring up feelings from both inside and outside the workplace. These powerful feelings often make it difficult for staff groups, however positively they view themselves, to change their patterns of verbal and non-verbal communication.

Any school is a complex organisation. Those working in it, caught up as they are in it's history and ways of doing things, are not always best placed to look clearly at those ways of doing things. Both strengths and weaknesses can be missed and opportunities for improvement lost.

For these reasons it is often desirable, though not always possible, for the consultant to work with someone from outside the school organisation. Such a person is in a position to 'make safe' a re-appraisal of approaches, of roles and of patterns of interaction among the staff in relation to the very emotive subject of managing behaviour. This does *not* have to be an intense or confrontational process. The fact that the person is an outsider who has taken a fresh look at the school's ways of doing things, combined with their hoped-for skill and experience, can enhance communication and the exploration of new approaches.

Often it is simply not possible to find a suitable outsider. This book can be used to help fill this gap and to make the task of the facilitator an easier one. By keeping the considerations raised in this section in mind the facilitator is in a better position to step back mentally and help the staff through times of difficulty. A significant part of the facilitator's task can then be to gently remind the group at appropriate times of it's contract to suspend disagreements and act together, the last of the Principles of the development structure.

The Working Party and Facilitator

It is often desirable for there to be a core group which brings together and represents the various roles of those working in the school. This group can oversee the work and help to ensure that it is seen as a collective effort.

In a primary school this group could include, if possible, a junior and infant classroom teacher, a member of the senior management team, a governor, a classroom assistant, the senior meals supervisor, a parent and the external consultant if one was being used. A school might also choose to involve others such as the secretary or schoolkeeper who, in some schools, have a great deal to do with the pupils and how they behave. The difficulties of getting all these roles together can often be overcome by finding people who perform more than one role.

A group of about eight people can usually accommodate the ranges of roles involved and ensure that there are always enough people present to make a viable meeting. On the other hand the group is not so large as to become unwieldy and inefficient. It is a task-orientated group and clear agendas, effective chairing and minutes will help maintain progress. **Discussion about behaviour can easily become anecdotal and concerned with immediate problems in the**

school. This can be informative as a starting point, but the group needs to be very careful not to become a talking shop.

The functions of the Working Party are to:

- Involve a full range of staff roles
- Provide and collate information and make it available to all staff
- Gather opinion and organise it's feedback
- Gather information from research and other schools
- Provide a forum for discussion of issues
- Present issues to the staff in a way that encourages positive discussion of differences
- Oversee the development process, keeping it to the agreed structure and timetable

The facilitator has a special role in this last respect. For this, he or she will need the support of the rest of the working party. The facilitator's role is to ensure that the working party itself is keeping to timetable. The facilitator will need to have a clear vision of the various stages and strands in the development process. This overall picture should be continuously communicated to and checked with other members of the Working Party so that at no time is the facilitator seen to have special knowledge. The danger of this would be that he or she could be perceived to be determining the content of the Policy.

Organisational and Secretarial Back-Up

Secretarial back-up should be identified at the outset because typed versions of discussions will be important to the process.

In line with the principle that all contributions will be valued and that discussions will result in something written, it is desirable for all contributions made by staff in paired discussion and by classes of pupils to be typed. **They are then kept in a central Behaviour Policy Development Folder in the staffroom.** A ring-binder is useful as it can be easily added to.

It is from these written contributions that the Policy itself is drafted, using the words in which the contributions were made. **If the contributions are given the recognition of being typed and well presented in a folder available to all, the status of all members of the school community is enhanced**. For non-teaching staff, to be given this sense of status and being taken seriously can produce subtle changes in self-image which can be of great benefit to the school in the long run.

The typing needs to be done quite promptly as the work progresses and the amount can be too great for individuals to cover in their spare time. It will be useful if the school secretary understands the full process to be gone through and is in a position to help the facilitator and working party with general organisational details and reminders.

Staff Training

A part of the development work will be to identify staff training needs in the management of behaviour, as individuals and as a team. This will need to reflect an integrated approach to staff functioning which incorporates *all* staff roles. A key area might be the management of behaviour at lunchtime. This involves enhancing the skills and status of mealtime supervisors *and* improving the communication between teaching and non-teaching staff. **There is a need in some schools for both separate training of non-teaching staff and joint training sessions for the whole staff.**

When looking at the training needs of non-teaching staff a number of considerations arise such as time worked, availability at staff-meeting times and their perceived status. It is important to recognise non-teaching staff training as a serious investment for the school and headteachers will need to allocate funding to this.

> *There is a need to face the issue of whether non-teaching staff should be paid to attend training sessions, just as teachers are. There will be a need for both separate and joint sessions. In a situation where joint training is a new practice there will be a training imbalance to address at this initial stage . In this situation the training needs of various sections of staff might not be met on a pro-rata basis.*

Staff Meetings

It can be useful to organise staff meetings to reflect the structure and strands of the development process and the principles outlined above. The rationale for doing this will need to be explained to staff as otherwise it might seem that opportunities for free discussion are being unreasonably curtailed. A place can be made for free discussion, but it is very important that all staff are actively involved in the process, that all contributions are valued and that discussions take place across the usual professional boundaries of teaching and non-teaching staff. **Tightly structured meetings, based mostly on pair or small group work, can help to ensure that the process reflects these principles.** An example is given in the section on Staff Responsibilities later in this chapter.

There needs to be a structure in which each person can feel comfortable about making a contribution and so actually does feel free to make one. This is different from the usual approach of ensuring that everyone '*has the opportunity....*' or is '*invited*' to contribute. There are a range of inhibiting factors that can come into play. These are, for example, differences in class, life and educational background, shyness about talking in a group, group dynamics and factional splits within the teaching and wider staff groups, and many others. Nevertheless, not everyone will want to contribute in an obvious way.

The structure suggested here is intended to mitigate human and institutional factors by keeping the tasks personal, practical and immediate. The context - a private discussion in a pair is as non-intimidatory as possible. By always having a written product which is reproduced and used to write the Policy, the pair members can see their contribution go forward into the Policy. The same issues apply to the Parents Meeting.

Structuring Staff Pairs

It might be useful to take a long-term view of this as the approach proposed could be useful in addressing other policies and purposes in the life of the school. It could be used for staff discussion or consultation over a wide range of issues and also as a way of addressing the non-communication between the many roles within the staff group. By giving very careful thought to a pair structure initially, a flexible and extremely useful tool can be created.

At the outset a list of pairs is drawn up which involves every member of the school staff. When doing this the pairs can be arranged so that teachers are paired with non-teachers where possible, senior management with others, splits and factions within the staff group are addressed and many other factors of gender, confidence, etc are also thought about. Careful thought must be given to ensuring that mid-day Supervisors who perform no other duties in the school can also be involved in the pair structure. It is best if this list is drawn up by a member of the senior management team or someone perceived by the staff as fair-minded and is then **viewed as non-negotiable.** It should be displayed clearly and everyone made aware of it or given copies.

Pair discussions need not only take place in staff meetings, but can also take place formally or informally at other times. It is sometimes best to ask staff, if the first pair meeting is outside a staff meeting, to just meet briefly and introduce themselves and undertake only one other task. Pair meetings can also take place at times of the day when most staff are free such as an assembly. Special assembly arrangements can even be made where the whole school assembly can be taken by a few people who then have their pair meetings at another time. **It is very useful if short written contributions from pairs are established from the outset as the norm.** It can be emphasised that these need only be brief notes.

In Chapter 6

We look at the practical application of these structures in the Primary School. Those wishing to apply them to involving the school community in the secondary sector will also find the chapter relevant.

---

5. INFORMATION GATHERING
– What You Need To Know

'We have observed that those schools which recognise that enquiry and reflection are important processes in school improvement find it easier to sustain improved effort around established priorities,and are better placed to monitor the extent to which policies actually deliver the intended outcomes for pupils...'

'Creating the conditions for school improvement - A Handbook of Staff Development Activities'
Ainscow, Hopkins, Southworth, West

Enquiry and Reflection

Information gathering and analysis is central to the process of any policy development. In Whole School Behaviour Policy development, information gathering and analysis can be instrumental in:

- identifying areas of concern
- engaging everybody in the process
- providing statistical baselines for subsequent comparison
- supporting decision making

Since every institution is unique, what follows constitutes a selection of the most commonly occurring issues and strategies encountered and is intended as a guide or basis for planning rather than an exhaustive inventory of points, pitfalls and pro-formas!

This chapter will focus on the ASSESSMENT stage of the 'R A F I E' model of analysis (described in the introduction). Accurate and appropriate information gathering, crucial to any type of assessment, contributes also to any interventions proposed.

The assessment techniques and tools used in the first stages of policy development are also valuable reassessment (evaluation) tools in subsequent stages and will provide further data for comparative and evaluative purposes.

Assessment

Existing documents and other sources of data can provide detailed information about:

- What is **currently happening** (e.g. consistency / awareness / effectiveness of existing procedures, structures, policies)
- What needs **to be changed**, introduced or developed further
- What needs **to be done next** (e.g. further assessment, monitoring, further information gathering, consultation)

It may be useful to consider drawing up **a checklist** outlining various sources of information / documents relevant to WSBP development that are available to the institution. This may include internal documents such as:

- Equal Opportunities policy
- Existent Code of Conduct
- Governors recommendations

The CODE OF CONDUCT

Be proud of your school
Be friendly to everyone
Do your best
Use your skills and abilities
Make the best of your time
Concentrate
Be self confident

A vague but positive set of rules.

The example here illustrates how useful it can be to examine existing documents. In this case there are a number of rather vague but positive statements to which it may be difficult to apply any success criteria and thus sanctions.

A checklist might also mention a variety of **other sources of data / information** for example:

- Exclusion figures
- SEN / pastoral records
- School handbook
- Pupil profiles

Documents or articles from **external sources** could also be included, for example:

- Elton report
- Other schools policies
- Training videos etc.

TYPES OF INFORMATION

An important avenue of enquiry will seek to determine **whether what is believed to be happening is in fact taking place**. Gathering information can provide an awareness of inconsistencies and provide the substance of further discussion. Thus two important areas of information gathering may be identified in:

- What people **think and feel** - perceptions / ideas / opinions / beliefs
- What people **actually do** - behaviour / systems / structures

The following points illustrate enquiries of this nature and the accompanying questions are simple examples which have informed debate.

- Issues of **consistency** - Do *all* class teachers complete a referral form each time a pupil is sent to the Head teacher?
- Are **structures** for communication effective - Do relevant Form Tutors receive a copy of referral forms initiated by Heads of Year?
- Are **systems** working effectively - Are racist incidents recorded centrally and followed up consistently?
- Are **rules** adhered to - Do all students wear correct school uniform?
- What **principles / ethos** are reflected in practice - Is there an effective system of rewards?

What people THINK and FEEL can be determined through discussion, structured and unstructured interviews, questionnaires, checklists etc. What people ACTUALLY DO can be determined through systematic observation techniques. The list above gives some idea of areas to explore and questions which could be posed. Individual institutions will need to devise their own programme, taking into account those areas / issues which perhaps:

- a majority feel to be important
- indicate an unacceptable gap between policy and practice
- have not been reviewed for some time...
- would enable new initiatives to be developed

Providing a clear focus for development

Areas needing to be investigated or developed may be identified in a number of ways, for example:

- The next phase in an Institutional Development / Management Plan
- Local or central government initiatives
- Recent conferences / training etc.
- Pupil concerns
- Parental or Governors' concerns
- Surveys or questionnaires of staff, pupils and parents

The NEW CODE OF CONDUCT

Be polite and helpful
Follow teachers' instructions
Bring the correct equipment
Sort out difficulties without fighting
Act safely
Wear school uniform

A reviewed Code of Conduct

Undergoing a process of full consultation is the most likely way to produce greatest coherence, consensus and commitment in practice as well as on paper in policy development! Once issues have been identified, appropriate information can be sought.

One school simply asked its staff to respond to the following:

What are your concerns re. behaviour in relation to:
    i)   the school - broad issues
    ii)   your faculty
    iii)   your classroom

It may be left to a **Working Party** or else to senior management to **prioritise concerns** and decide which methods of assessment would be the most appropriate and practical ways to gather the necessary information.

Assessment techniques

SYSTEMATIC OBSERVATION might well be considered to be too time consuming for the purposes of behaviour policy development. It might also be thought that to shadow or observe teachers directly could be construed negatively and therefore ultimately might prove counterproductive. Nevertheless some schools may find it possible for teachers to collaborate in producing an observation schedule with a specific and positive bias in order to identify successful classroom management strategies. This would provide useful feedback and contribute to the dissemination of good practice.

A focus of an observation schedule might include:

- The clarity of instructions
- The effectiveness of routines
- The effects of ignoring calling out
- The effectiveness of setting time limits
- The effective use of praise - public / private
- Pupil contact rate
- Numbers of positive / negative interactions
- Numbers of pupil-initiated / teacher-initiated interactions

PUPIL SHADOWING accompanied by structured questionnaires was found both practical and useful. Thus direct observation could be compared directly with pupil perception.

Pupil Shadowing Questionnaire

1) How clear were you about the aims of the lesson?

2) Were you able to understand the teachers' explanations of the work?

3) Could you read the material used by the teachers?

4) Were you able to get the teacher's attention when you needed it?

5) Were you able to concentrate during the lesson?

6) Did you use any of the following during the lesson:
   a) A text book
   b) A worksheet
   c) Audio-visual equipment
   d) Other

7) Did you work in any of the following ways:
   a) By yourself
   b) As a group
   c) Taught as a class

STRUCTURED QUESTIONNAIRES and CHECKLISTS FOR INTERVIEW are useful because it is possible to:

- take an identified area / issue and then to formulate a series of questions or statements which are generated to explore relevant variables.
- trial the questionnaire with a small sample group to identify problems / areas needing further development.
- take further samples on subsequent occasions for a satisfactory sample size to be agreed / achieved.
- show successive drafts to relevant / interested people so that final format / content is agreed by all concerned.
- provide a method of investigation which with some simple guidelines, allows any member of staff to conduct the interviews / questionnaires and maintain consistency of delivery.
- ensure that the nature of response categories are simple and easy to mark without misleading interpretation. Thus, marking, collation and feedback of data can be kept relatively simple and accurate.

QUESTIONNAIRES - MAXIMISING AN ACCURATE and FULL RESPONSE

There are various ways respondents can indicate a preference, an opinion etc. In response to a question such as:

Do you use rewards?

the simplest may be

Yes / No

However:

Never / Occasionally / Fairly often / Very often

provides a broader range of response which may offer more useful results.

In addition to this, a checklist indicating alternatives can invite the respondent not only to indicate, for example, which rewards they may use, but perhaps also to reflect upon a broader range of rewards than they might otherwise consider. Such checklists can be drawn up from the range of possibilities known to be in use generally and may also include additional ideas from other sources (institutions / books etc). By augmenting the potentially available repertoire of the individual, it may sometimes be possible to make suggestions, fuel debate and influence practice. Thus, assessment slips into intervention - albeit indirectly and informally!

It is likely that respondents will answer honestly and openly, questions in print, which they would not necessarily answer in the same way in a face to face interview! This applies both to adults and to pupils.

A very useful response format is to offer a continuum which is marked as desired: Such formats offer the opportunity for numerical scoring and later comparisons.

BEHAVIOUR POLICY QUESTIONNAIRE

Are you: Early Years   (KS 1)   KS 2   SMT

Please indicate how true you think the following statements are. Add comments as appropriate.

1 = Not at all true   5 = Completely true

1) The school has a clearly defined discipline structure which enables me to gain support if I need it
    1   2   (3)   4   5

2) As a staff we respond consistently to incidents of poor in-class behaviour   *differences between classes*
    1   (2)   3   4   5   *and KS's*

3) There is a particular range of strategies for dealing with poor behaviour that the school encourages
    1   2   3   (4)   5   *Not always used!*

4) I feel able to seek practical, informal support from colleagues when dealing with disruptive behaviour
    1   2   3   4   (5)

Tallies of scores from each question can then be made to identify areas of concern:

1)	1	2	3	4	5		2)	1	2	3	4	5
	/	9	10	3	—			9	9	2	2	—

3)	1	2	3	4	5		4)	1	2	3	4	5
	1	—	6	12	3			—	—	—	9	13

5)	1	2	3	4	5		6)	1	2	3	4	5

All such response designs have the potential advantages of:
- being easy and fast to complete
- stimulating easily collatable and comparable data
- promoting clear unambiguous responses
- reducing superfluous / unfocussed data
- being easily reproduced for later comparison / evaluation

For ease of use and to minimise the time and effort involved, try not to let your questionnaires:
- be verbose or too long (people are busy!)
- have too broad a focus
- contain too many open-ended questions (hard to collate)

It is important to write questionnaires with the particular audience in mind. Using technical language for those unfamiliar to it such as pupils or non-teaching staff can seriously inhibit responses. Even if respondents are familiar with it, jargon is frequently found to be unpopular and so could affect the likelihood of full and candid answers.

Remember too that speakers of languages other than English, particularly parents, may appreciate translations into their mother tongue.

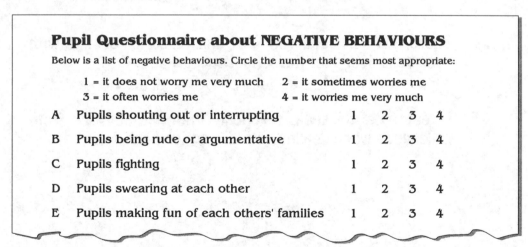

Pupil Questionnaire about NEGATIVE BEHAVIOURS

Below is a list of negative behaviours. Circle the number that seems most appropriate:

1 = it does not worry me very much   2 = it sometimes worries me
3 = it often worries me   4 = it worries me very much

A	Pupils shouting out or interrupting	1	2	3	4
B	Pupils being rude or argumentative	1	2	3	4
C	Pupils fighting	1	2	3	4
D	Pupils swearing at each other	1	2	3	4
E	Pupils making fun of each others' families	1	2	3	4

One school gave questionnaires to pupils, staff and parents about Positive Behaviours and Negative Behaviours. An extract of the pupil questionnaire is above. Some of the collated results are below.

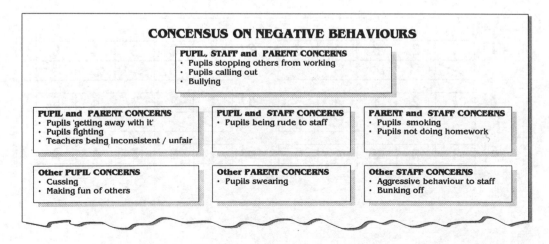

CONCENSUS ON NEGATIVE BEHAVIOURS

PUPIL, STAFF and PARENT CONCERNS
- Pupils stopping others from working
- Pupils calling out
- Bullying

PUPIL and PARENT CONCERNS
- Pupils 'getting away with it'
- Pupils fighting
- Teachers being inconsistent / unfair

PUPIL and STAFF CONCERNS
- Pupils being rude to staff

PARENT and STAFF CONCERNS
- Pupils smoking
- Pupils not doing homework

Other PUPIL CONCERNS
- Cussing
- Making fun of others

Other PARENT CONCERNS
- Pupils swearing

Other STAFF CONCERNS
- Aggressive behaviour to staff
- Bunking off

Some issues to consider when using questionnaires

Open-ended versus Closed questions

Open-ended questions such as *'What concerns about behaviour do you have?'* are effective at identifying the areas to focus on. Closed questions are useful for gathering facts about identified areas. Open-ended questions are generally harder to collate. Closed questions can often be scored.

Impartiality

One of the strengths of using an outside consultant to gather information within an institution is that they are more likely to be seen to be impartial to the institutions processes and politics. Thus it could be argued that the information gathered could be more accurate and revealing. In situations such as these it is important to differentiate between genuine and relevant grievances as opposed to those which are an expression of a more general disaffection and where it is apparent that a commitment to contribute positively and constructively to change is absent.

Structured interviews can minimise this possibility and allow the outside consultant to more easily guard against becoming a focus for, or mechanism through which, disaffection can be indirectly voiced.

Confidentiality

Confidentiality means that data is only accessible to pre-agreed individuals. Similarly analysis and feedback of the data should ensure that individuals cannot be linked to specific pieces of information. Outside consultants may be perceived to facilitate this more easily.

Anonymity

Complete anonymity may be difficult to guarantee if, for example the respondents were a small and specific sample group:

- *Year 8 girls referred by their Head of Year on more than four occasions.*
- *Representatives of a School Council*

Time

Some considerations which are relevant include:

- It is a time consuming exercise to design a questionnaire from scratch - so customise the ideas in this book.
- Collating can take time; computers are not always reliable or available when you need them!
- Optical marking is expensive unless you're thinking in large numbers! Collating by hand can drive you crazy!
- Sample sizes / group composition must be large enough / sufficiently representative to ensure accountability of results.
- Time-tabling needs careful planning for observations / interviews / questionnaires

- Pre-existing meetings / INSET timetables may impinge on everyone's time / patience / goodwill.
- Whether people can be released from the timetable to conduct observations / interviews or questionnaires.
- and effort....

In other words, does the information gained as a result of your enquiry justify the method time and effort put into it? This is largely a question of **establishing priorities** and having a clear idea exactly:

- **WHAT information you need**
- **HOW it will finally be used**

These need to be identified and agreed by all parties **before** any work begins.

Finally...

When gathering information in order to build upon good practice and to make an assessment of your current situation it may be prudent to remember to:

ACCENTUATE the POSITIVE!!

Whilst we may remember this for our pupils, we often forget it for ourselves and our colleagues.

DON'T BE RELUCTANT TO:
- Find out what **is already working well** - eg. systems / rules / structures etc.
- Determine **why it is working well** eg. consistency / shared purpose / intrinsically rewarding etc.
- **Look outside** your own institution for ideas

... and don't forget that...

- Solutions are not always portable....
- There is no merit in persistently reinventing the wheel!
- If things are working well they do not necessarily need to be changed!
- Creative solutions do not always start with blank pages!

Having fun in the play-ground

POSITIVE STRATEGIES QUESTIONNAIRE

Key Stage [2]

Indicate the frequency used: 1 = Never 3 = Sometimes 5 = Frequently

1) Have you developed your class rules in conjunction with your students?
Are they on show? *YES and ILLUSTRATED !!*
Do you refer to them when dealing with misbehaviour? -
I use them as a form of non-verbal reminder

2) What low-level behaviour management strategies do you use?

The Look! *5*   Proximity *5*   Refocusing *5*   *, I try to!*
Simple directions *4*   Diversions *4*   Avoiding using the word 'No' *2*
Non-verbal signals *3*   Giving a choice *3 4* Cool off time
Rule reminders *3*   Take-up Time *5*   Out-of-class Time Out *2*
In-class Time Out *2*   Giving a warning of a consequence *3*
Others: *When all else fails - use the thumb screws*
with Anne's class.

3) What positive strategies do you use? *Never as often as I'd like*

Non-verbal approval *3*   Verbal approval / acknowledgement *3*
Smiley faces *4*   Wall chart for positive behaviours *2*
Stamps *1*   Stickers *2*   Certificates *1*
Send to colleague *3*   Letters home *2*   Choosing time *2*
Individual rewards *3*   Class rewards *2*   Posts of responsibility *2*
Individual 'Good books' *2*   Class 'Good Book' ✓   School Council Rep ✓
Send to phase coodinator / HT   Public recognition
Others: *2*   *Particularly for LOP 2-3*

4) What routines / procedures do you use for avoiding difficulties?
Line up in table-group order.

5) What activities do you use for raising self-esteem / confidence / self-awareness etc   *, also curriculum work.*

Circle work *- weekly*   Developing the language of feelings
Listening skills   Role-play ⟷   Assertiveness skills
Sharing skills   News   Conflict resolution skills
Others: *at register time*   *3-step technique*

Example of a questionnaire which provides opportunities for marking suggested responses at the same time as providing spaces for the respondent to add their own comments and ideas. Most people find underlining responses manageable; some may feel that writing is too demanding.

---

6. DEVELOPING A PRIMARY BEHAVIOUR POLICY

Introduction

This chapter is about putting the structures outlined in Chapter 4 into practice in the primary school. It provides a detailed, step-by-step guide to *one approach* to developing a Primary Behaviour Policy. Many of the strategies proposed can also be used in the secondary setting.

This approach may not be the one best-suited to the needs of your school. The purpose is not to provide a blueprint, though it can be used that way. The aim is:

- To put forward a way of thinking in detail about implementation.
- To keep the considerations of involving the school community always in mind.
- To enable the reader to draw out ideas and practice which suit their needs.

This chapter is divided into three sections:

    1. Staff Tasks   2. Work with the Pupils   3. The Parents' Meeting

1. Staff Tasks - *A Practical Guide*

The three activities within the staff group are to write following sections of the Policy:

- **The Staff Responsibilities**
- **Encouraging and Acknowledging Good Behaviour**
- **The Hierarchy of Sanctions**

In the pairs work and staff meetings these three activities are taken forward concurrently. What follows is a list of tasks in time order. This list and the order it has been put in might seem detailed and prescriptive but is intended as a framework which can be adapted to the needs of your school.

The Working Party Tasks

The Working Party (WP) will be co-ordinating a wide range of activities. Staying on task, good chairing, careful time keeping and actioned minutes will be important. WP Tasks might be:

- To read the Introduction to this book and familiarise themselves with the **'Timetable for Developing a Behaviour Policy'** and other materials in this chapter. Alternatively they could divide up the reading, but the Facilitator should be familiar with all of it. If the WP, the lead body in the process, is always clear about what is happening and why, the development will go much more smoothly.

- If the **Governors** are not already involved, deciding how this is to be done.

- To arrange for the drawing up of a list of **staff pairs**. To co-ordinate the next Pairs Tasks, produce instructions for them and duplicate these. To arrange how and when the Pairs Tasks take place, whether informally or at a designated time. (See pages 40-41)

- To outline the initiative at a **teaching staff meeting** and ensure that all other staff are aware of it. If pairs are to be used before the first whole staff meeting, outline to staff the rationale for how these have been drawn up and how they are to be used.

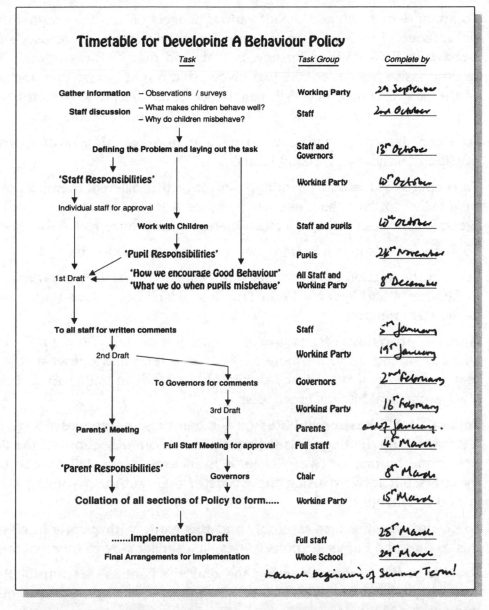

Timetable for Developing A Behaviour Policy

Task		Task Group	Complete by
Gather information	– Observations / surveys	**Working Party**	2nd September
Staff discussion	– What makes children behave well? – Why do children misbehave?	**Staff**	2nd October
	Defining the Problem and laying out the task	**Staff and Governors**	13th October
	'Staff Responsibilities'	**Working Party**	6th October
Individual staff for approval			
	Work with Children	**Staff and pupils**	6th October
	'Pupil Responsibilities'	**Pupils**	24th November
1st Draft	**'How we encourage Good Behaviour'** **'What we do when pupils misbehave'**	**All Staff and Working Party**	8th December
To all staff for written comments		**Staff**	5th January
	2nd Draft	**Working Party**	19th January
	To Governors for comments	**Governors**	2nd February
	3rd Draft	**Working Party**	16th February
Parents' Meeting		**Parents**	end of January.
	Full Staff Meeting for approval	**Full staff**	4th March
'Parent Responsibilities'	**Governors**	**Chair**	8th March
Collation of all sections of Policy to form.....		**Working Party**	15th March
.......Implementation Draft		**Full staff**	25th March
Final Arrangements for Implementation		**Whole School**	28th March

Launch beginning of Summer Term!

This Timetable shows the flow of work to be undertaken throughout the development process described in this chapter. It leads to a Draft Policy for implementation. This includes sections on Staff, Pupil and Parent Responsibilities. It also includes sections on the proposed structures for encouraging good behaviour and responding to misbehaviour. The Timetable is intended as a planning document. The group with overall responsibility for each activity is shown, together with a target date for completion of the activity. It would be useful if all staff had a copy of the Timetable and it was displayed in the staffroom.

- **To gather information** – especially about the concerns of members of staff – this could be a Pairs exercise to take place before the first staff meeting, though whether to use the Pairs in this way before there is the chance to explain them fully to the assembled staff is a matter of judgement.

- To prepare the central **Behaviour Policy Development Folder** - a ring binder with dividers is the most practical. This enables different aspects of the work to be put in sections such as Minutes, Agendas, Feedback from Pairs, Parents, Work with the Pupils, Feedback from Pupils, Working Party Papers, Information Collected, Policy Examples, etc. The purpose is for all aspects of the work to be easily and quickly accessible to all staff.

- To arrange for small sections of various aspects of the development work to be videoed. This leaves open various possibilities for future use, such as a **Behaviour Policy Video** for new parents and pupils. The purpose would be to emphasise how everyone was involved. It might be useful to include clips of the staff meeting, the WP, pairs discussion, the launch assembly for the pupils and their work in the classrooms, the Parents' meeting, etc.

- To clarify issues around how to include **non-teaching staff** in meetings outside their normal working hours.

- **To prepare for the staff meeting.** It might be that different members of the WP might want to share the presentation of their work and the development process proposed. This can make for a more interesting and varied feel to the meeting.

- To arrange the smooth running of the **secretarial back-up**.

- Look at the section on *'Principles and Practice for the Development Process'* in Chapter 4 and **agree a Main Principle** which could be suggested to staff at the staff meeting.

- **Agree a provisional timetable** and mark this on the 'Timetable' - the time allowed should be somewhere between one term and one year. There is no real reason why a Draft Policy should not be ready in one term, but there are always practical hitches in schools!

- **To draft Staff Responsibilities** into fifteen or so sentences using the Pairs feedback. The drafting, as is the case with the other Sections of the Policy, is best done by one or two people. It is an exercise in skilfully combing the thoughts put forward using the words of their authors. Nothing should be added or changed.

- To co-ordinate the first assembly and **the work with pupils** in class. After this to draft the Pupils Responsibilities, in a similar way to those of the Staff.

- To arrange **the Parents Meeting** and draft the Parents' Responsibilities. (The draft might be done by the Head.) To put up the display of Parents' work done at the Meeting.

There will be many other tasks for members of the Working Party as the work progresses. The above is intended to get the group started.

Tasks at the First Staff Meeting

Please bear in mind the comments made in the section of Chapter 4 entitled *'Staff Meetings'* and *'Structuring Staff Pairs'* and consider the idea for a group presentation to staff by the WP. The tasks are:

- Refer to the principles on which the work will be based,

- Display and talk through the *'Timetable for Development of a Behaviour Policy'* (consider copying enough of these for each member of staff to have one).

- Outline any Information Gathering to date.

- Say something about the role of the Governors or ask a Governor present to do this.

- Display the Behaviour Policy Development Folder and say where in the Staffroom this will be kept.

- Explain how the WP was selected by roles and the choice of Facilitator.

- Explain fully how and why staff were paired and how the Staff Pairs will be used.

- Stress the need for brief and legible notes from each discussion.

- After a five minute brainstorm, recorded for typing-up on a flip-chart, on *'What Makes Pupils Behave Well'*, introduce the first Pairs Task.

> *Nazmi and Roger.*
> 3.   *For individual Pupils we.......*
>   *Have computer time at the end of day.*
>   *Praise in Assembly etc.*
>   *For classes we.......*
>   *Have choosing time on Friday, etc.*
>
> 4.   *In class we shall have......*
>   *Time Out...... etc.*

- Ask people to put their names on their sheets and put the Pairs Task number clearly on the Sheet.

- Each idea should be on a separate line. All this makes typing of a large amount of feedback far quicker.

- As can be seen, the answers will come in various permutations. You might wish to concentrate on particular aspects at first (eg classroom, playground, individual, or class) or just see what comes up.

- In the Pairs Task after the Brainstorm it might be worth posing the question suggested on the Agenda in order to get staff thinking about a Hierarchical approach to sanctions.

Three points about this meeting:

- **It's success will depend on it being well chaired** so that the tasks are achieved smoothly in the times allocated.

- **Tight chairing will necessitate curtailing general discussion.** General discussion and airing of feelings is NOT the purpose of the meeting. Instead, it is part of a building process in which *everyone* will be constructively heard.

- **At a later stage it might be appropriate for the whole staff to discuss potentially divisive issues such as rewards and sanctions.** The structure is designed to make the discussion, when it comes, a productive one rather than one which becomes heated, semantic and unnecessarily divisive. Such discussions in the opening stages can rob the work of momentum.

Pairs Tasks

The nature of these and the rationale for them, were discussed in Chapter 4. Whenever Pairs discussions take place **instructions should be clear and specific.** It is productive to ask Pairs to make **a small number** of suggestions within each task, rather than making an unlimited request. For example, *'Three Things We Do Already...'* The task then feels short and specific. Instructions should preferably be **written** whether the Pairs activity is within or outside delegated meeting time. It might be worth varying the time these discussions take place, so as not to place a strain on either the 'free time' of staff members or meeting time available.

Here is a list of some of the tasks which Pairs could undertake as time goes on. These represent the discussions to which everyone on the staff should contribute.

- Listing the particular concerns of individual staff members about behaviour in the classroom and across the school. This could happen before or at the first staff meeting.

- Writing the *Staff Responsibilities*. At first staff meeting.

- *Five Things We Do Already To Encourage Good Behaviour.* At first staff meeting.

- *Five Things We Do Already When Pupils Misbehave.* At first staff meeting.

- List Behaviours which are *Minor, Moderately Serious, Very Serious.* Or, as an alternative task, they could be asked to consider how the school should respond to these levels of behaviour and also to repeated Minor misbehaviour. (See Chapters 2 and 11)

First Draft - Behaviour Policy   To all staff.

STAFF RESPONSIBILITIES

- In your pairs could you please discuss what you think are the Staff Responsibilities regarding behaviour in the school. These are the responsibilities towards the pupils of all the adults working in the school, whether they are teachers, support staff, meals supervisors, school secretary, schoolkeeper or any other adult having some dealings with the pupils.

- Please write 3 sentences to outline what you think are the most important responsibilities.

- These contributions will then be typed up and put in the Behaviour Policy Development Folder in the staffroom. From them 15 sentences will be written including as many of the main points as possible and staying as close as possible to the original wording.

- This will then be displayed for all staff working in the school to see and if there are no objections to the way everyone's ideas have been combined it will become the Staff Responsibilities section of the school Behaviour Policy.

- *Three Things We Could Do To Encourage Pupils to Behave Well* - as individuals or classes, in the classroom and across the school. In this and the following task staff should consider how their suggestions would mesh with current practice.

- *Three Things We Could Do If Pupils Misbehave* - a Hierarchy of sanctions.

- Some responses to the WP Draft Document - when these responses are typed up the WP could use them to prepare amendments to their draft in light of the comments received. This activity is to prepare for a staff meeting to discuss and ratify the Draft Policy.

- *Encouraging Good Behaviour* - some responses to the WP Draft of this section. The Draft is similarly amended by the WP in light of comments before the ratification Staff Meeting.

2. The Pupils' Responsibilities

The aim is to involve the pupils in such a way that:

- They become interested in considering the way they behave
- They become, and then remain, involved in formulating and implementing the Policy
- Their involvement is *active*
- The written Policy *visibly* contains their input
- There is a thread running from their original input to the activities involved in the implementation of the Policy
- These threads are communicated to them by the staff and *make sense* to them
- The Responsibilities they identify replace written rules as far as possible

Steps in the Process

1. **First Assembly** The Policy Development process is presented

2. **Work in Class** Work takes place in all classes across the school within the same day as the Launch Assembly. The pupil's ideas are recorded on paper in their own words

3. **The Pupils' Responsibilities** are drafted using their words

4. These are presented to an Assembly - displays of all the work done in class

5. **The Policy Launch Assembly** The Policy is launched for implementation

6. **Implementation** Aspects of the implementation are based directly on the *'Pupils' Responsibilities'* section of the Policy

The First Assembly

This assembly needs to be interesting. If it incorporates some drama, role playing or some other visual device, possibly with humour, all the better. It should be remembered! The involvement of everyone in the school community should be stressed and how hard each group is going to be working. The message is twofold:

- The pupils' opinions matter and are valued

- The pupils' opinions, as well as those of staff and parents, will be *acted on*

Work in the Classroom

Some schools have chosen to **devote a morning** to this so that the work in class can follow directly on from the Launch Assembly while the topic is still fresh in the pupils' minds. **This allocation of valuable time recognises the central importance of behaviour to successful curriculum delivery.** Doing it this way also makes the administration of the whole exercise more straightforward and in this way can be time-saving. If this is not possible, it is best that **all the work takes place on the same day.** The idea is to generate discussion amongst the pupils and a sense of communal purpose that extends beyond the individual classroom.

It is important that teachers are given **clear, written guidelines** of what is required. Experience suggests that where this is not done there are inevitably time-wasting misunderstandings. For instance: a class where each pupil produced a great deal of written work, but there wasn't a summing up session. The result was unmanageable for typing! Or a class which did excellent drama for a whole session, but nothing was recorded. Remember to **video** some of the work in class!

A sample of guidelines for class teachers could look like this:

<u>First Draft - Behaviour Policy</u>

To all Class Teachers:

PUPILS' RESPONSIBILITIES

Our aim is to include a section in the policy on the Pupils's Responsibilities, to be written in their own words. Please take the themes introduced in assembly and take them forward in work with your class on the same day.

Examples of the form this work can take are:

> writing   role plays   drama   painting   brainstorms
> ... and can be done as you think appropriate in groups or with the whole class.

Please bring the class back together at the end to share the work that they've done. As they give this feedback PLEASE RECORD ON A LARGE PIECE OF PAPER A LIST OF THEIR RESPONSES USING EXACTLY THEIR OWN WORDS. (If the class activity was a brainstorm please record this in the same way.) These will be typed up and will be used to write the *'Pupils' Responsibilities'*.

When all the class contributions are typed, the Pupils' Responsibilities are drafted by the Working Party using the pupils' own words. Nothing is changed or added.

The Policy Launch Assembly

If the draft Policy in it's entirety is not going to be ready for a long time it might be best to show the pupils the completed *'Pupils' Responsibilities'* at a separate assembly, with displays of the work done in the classes and possibly some of the drama from those classes which chose to work that way. The pupil's then see the fruits of their labours while it is still fresh in their minds.

If the draft is ready, then the full Policy Launch Assembly can take place. It can be helpful, where there has already been an earlier assembly, the pupils work is nevertheless again displayed, along with some of the work by staff and parents. The Behaviour Policy Development Folder might also be shown, pointing to the section with the typed results of each class's work! **One aim of the assembly is to give the feel of something that has resulted from communal labour in which the pupils have taken a valued part.**

Implementation

Wherever possible, **structure the work done by the pupils in this development phase into the day-to-day implementation of the finished Policy.** This can be done in a number of ways.

An example of this is where the **'Pupils's Responsibilities' are used to provide weekly or fortnightly themes for behaviour effort in the school.** One Responsibility is taken as the theme, displayed in the hall and in classrooms and is used or referred to in class discussions and work. **Systems for encouraging good behaviour can then be built around this theme where recognition is given at an individual and class.** This has worked very successfully in schools and the popularity of the systems with pupils seems to last over long periods of time. Systems include a weekly Behaviour Assembly, class and school Helpful and Friendly Trees, stickers and Good Behaviour Books. Different forms of recognition will suit different schools.

The effect is that the pupils see the their work, presented in their own words, being used as a cornerstone of the running of the school. With this comes a sense of value. And of Responsibility!

3. The Parents' Meeting

This is a structured, task-orientated meeting with a representative group of parents who are personally invited to attend. The purpose of the meeting is NOT to have an open discussion or to elicit and listen to parental views. The purpose is for the parents present to carry out the very specific task of writing down the Parents' Responsibilities.

It is important that the parents selected to discuss the 'Parents Responsibilities' is seen to be fair and impartial. One way is as follows: The parents of the 10th child on the register of each class in the school are invited. As it is best to invite about 16 parents, you might choose in a small school to invite the parents of both the 10th and 20th child on each register. This must be done without any variation, no matter which

---

parents are chosen as a result, because it is often very important to those present that they have been fairly chosen.

Sometimes the experience of schools is that parents do not attend parents meetings in other than very small numbers. This expectation should be put to one side.

- Parents are **individually** and **personally** invited during the week or two preceding the meeting and it is explained how and why they have been **chosen** and the importance of the contribution they are being asked to make to the school.

- Where the parents of the 10th child are unable to attend, those of the 11th should be invited, and so on.

- It is helpful if the meeting can be arranged at a time suitable to most parents.

- It is most practical if the class teachers who see the parents on a regular basis in a primary school can give out the bulk of the invitations as they are also well placed to provide the **essential** reminder on the day before the meeting and the day of the meeting.

Meetings approached in this way usually result in the nearly full attendance of those invited.

It might be helpful to have an outside consultant to chair the meeting for parents as it can avoid inappropriate parental expectations of the meeting.

The meeting should be tightly chaired and its purposes and limitations outlined very clearly at the beginning. As the meeting is entirely about tasks performed by pairs who will share opinions between themselves and then with other pairs, any **general discussion should be very gently but extremely firmly stopped.** The fact that this is a working meeting and the importance and honour of representing the parents in drafting their Policy should be stressed. The impartiality of the method used to choose parental representatives needs to be stressed.

Careful planning should supplement careful structuring of the Parents' meeting. Teachers are used to laying out their contributions, but the object here is to get a group who have never performed these tasks to do them naturally, easily and with results that look clear and well-ordered. We are asking a group who, in some cases, might not even be fully literate or have English as their first language, to both formulate a policy and to participate in the *making* of the presentation. The point of this is **to ensure that the experience is of a real involvement.**

Running the Meeting

The Parents' Meeting Agenda has a column for approximate **timings** and another for the person introducing each item.

In the meeting shown the headteacher would introduce the aims and outline exactly how the parents were **chosen**. In this case, the outside consultant being used, would introduce himself and then outline in what would happen at various the **stages** of the meeting.

17.5.95

Dear Yvonne,

I enclose an Agenda, which we can talk about. Also a sample letter to parents as discussed. The **creche** is an optional extra which we can think about - maybe it's not necessary? What follows is a checklist, but we can talk again nearer the time.

You need for the meeting:

    4 - 5 interpreters

    Someone to do the tea half way

    Copy of the Policy to date

    File of materials accumulated during the development

    Pens / pencils

    3 sheets of sugar paper

    5 Pritt sticks

    Plain chocolate biscuits for a break half-way

    Some strips of paper for parents to write their ideas on

Look forward to it.

A letter from a consultant to a headteacher

The headteacher would then briefly show the parents the **Behaviour Policy Development Folder** from the staffroom and indicate the work being done by staff and pupils on the Policy. The point is to emphasise that everyone is working together on this endeavour rather than to show the details of any of the work done so far.

The consultant would then describe the Policy that was being drafted, and go on to talk about the **School Code** and the Staff Responsibilities section, which would have been completed by then. The headteacher would then talk about the experience of the **Working Party** and the principles underlying the work being done in the school. She would then go on to talk about the last two sections of the Policy, on **Encouraging Good Behaviour** and on the **Consequences of Misbehaviour.**

The consultant would then use

Activity

You have 15 minutes for the first bit of this activity.

Discuss with your partner what you regard as *a parent's responsibility for their child's behaviour at school.*

You will be put into 'Pairs' and given some strips of paper.

Agree which three ideas you want to record and write them down on three of the paper strips.

You will then move onto the next part of the activity for which you will also have 15 minutes.

You will get together with another 'Pair' and look at each other's ideas that have been written on the strips of paper. When you have discussed them in your 'Four' arrange them into a pyramid with the most important at the top and the least important at the base. You can stick them down with the glue provided.

At the end of this activity, there will be an opportunity for everyone to see the completed pyramids.

Alastair Ross 61

Green Fields Primary School Behaviour Policy

Parents Meeting   19.6.95

(Time in mins)			Intro'd by:

1.10   Introduction: Aim of the meeting is for parents to write   HT
the Parents' Responsibilities section of the Policy.

    How parents were chosen   C

    Previous schools, AR's role (Independent status), etc.

    Structure of the meeting   C

2. 2   Brief look at the school Policy Development Folder / materials   HT

    5   The Policy :   How it is being drafted   C

        School code

        Staff Responsibilities (if done)

        End section: WP + development   HT

        experience so far.

        Principles

3. 3   Staff Responsibilities: C

4. 15   Pairs: 'The three most important responsibilities a

    parent has about their children's behaviour at school'   C

  Write down on blanks.

    (In this group will be people who have problems reading and certainly writing
    - make them feel OK about this / have scribes)

5.15   Fours: Arrange as a Pyramid.   C

    (3 layers, if some are the same glue 2 together at the l-h end)

6. 5   Feedback + any objections to specific suggestions.   C

7.15   Prioritise in full group - (optional - see notes)   C

    Paste pyramid, put group names on sheets

8. 5   Procedure from here. To be ready in 2 weeks.   HT

HT will choose 10 items and will combine where appropriate **using Parents' own words.**

    Draft will be displayed with original pyramids in entrance hall.

    Parents check and sign if agree that it is a fair combination of points made.

---

    75 min

        Possibility of this group taking part in the Policy Review.

the 'Staff Responsibilities' section to introduce the first pairs task. It would be very important to reassure people that writing, spelling and presentation are not what this exercise is about. This would be done light heartedly and jokes about teachers who can't spell wouldn't be out of place. The consultant would then explain the activity. See the activity sheet for details of the process.

As with staff, **pairs should be chosen by the headteacher rather than the parents.**

The meeting is finished off by a promise that in two weeks the headteacher or another will have made a list of 10 sentences combining the Responsibilities written on the pyramids using the parents own words and bearing in mind the priority given to different items by the group. It is explained that this draft will be displayed along with the original pyramids at a suitable place in the school. Next to it there will be a list of those who attended with a request for them to sign or tick off their name if they agree that the sentences represent a fair combination of the points made on the pyramids.

Extending the Role of Parents

The Head Teacher also has the option to, when praising the group for their very successful work in the meeting, invite them to take part in a Review of the Policy at a later stage. This group of parents can then form a core group and meetings can be built into the review process within the school.

The group could thus become one forum for review of the Policy. At that stage it might be appropriate to have meetings of a looser format where views can be gathered and exchanged, possibly with the option of the group consulting other parents. This might seem the wrong way round to do things, gathering views after the fact, but the aim of the initial meeting is to immediately engage the parents in a meaningful way with a visible outcome – to leave those present with a sense of being actively useful. From this sense of value and genuine involvement, other tasks can be undertaken. In some cases further meetings are suggested by the parents themselves and it is worth making space for this eventuality.

This structure for consulting parents and gaining their active involvement can obviously be built on and extended into other Policy developments and school issues. By simply choosing a different number on the register and inviting that small group of parents to a meeting another core group can be formed which can be encouraged to meet periodically over time. It is a question of making the parents in the group feel valued and useful in being genuinely consulted and seeing the visible results of their efforts.

Concluding Remarks

This chapter has been very detailed. As I said at the beginning, the intention was to provide one example of a detailed approach to looking at the *practice* of developing a Behaviour Policy. Individual schools can then adapt the approaches and ideas to suit their needs.

7. ORGANISING POLICY DEVELOPMENT IN SECONDARY SCHOOLS

The Elton Report and the Whole School Behaviour Policy:

The policy should be grounded ....

extracting the approach to behaviour from documentation e.g. Elton Report and DFE circulars. The policy should be based on the Elton Report and DFE circulars that refer to Whole School Behaviour Policy development.

The Elton Report [1989] makes a number of points which need to be considered when developing a policy:

- It regards most behaviour problems as minor but that their cumulative effect can be a source of stress for teachers
- It sees violence against teachers as relatively rare in schools
- It states that there are no simple or complete solutions to behaviour problems
- It regards the school ethos as well as home background as influencing behaviour
- It suggests that the SMT should take the lead in developing policies
- It emphasizes positive behaviour /shared values / consensus on behaviour
- It suggests a Code of Conduct should be devised which should be supported by a system of rewards and sanctions
- It suggests a balance of rewards and sanctions
- It suggests that effective classroom and group behaviour management reduces disruptive behaviour
- It suggests that effective behaviour management can be learned
- It suggests whole school policies can enable teachers to be consistent in dealing with behaviour problems
- It encourages whole school community participation in policy development: parents / carers, governors, teaching and non-teaching staff and pupils.

WSBP Working Party: advantages, composition, aims, procedures, processes, decision-making and data collection.

The advantage of a WSBP working party is that it serves as a:

- means of co-ordination and dissemination
- forum for discussion
- means of involving a range of staff roles

The Composition of a WSBP Working Party:

It should have representative range of staff, teaching and non-teaching e.g. from the SMT, HOYs, HODs, NQTs, schoolkeeping, mealtime supervisors and office staff.

- led by a Deputy Head with heads of year and departments, teachers from each department including NQTs and schoolkeeping and office staff.
- governors should take an active role in policy development

The Aims of the WSBP Working Party:

The aims should be specific and clearly stated eg to assist in:

- formulating
- implementing
- evaluating

a whole school policy on behaviour.

The Procedures and Processes of the WSBP Working Party:

The working party should establish:

- How policy development Is to proceed e.g. in stages or holistically
- Whether to implement the policy on completion or to implement elements of the policy as they arise
- The time frame for formulation, implementation and evaluation
- The behavioural priorities for their institution, based on the opinion of the whole school community
- Ways of involving the whole school community
- What aspects does there need to be data on e.g. attendance, exclusions, staff and pupils' perceptions of behaviour, referral rooms, referral systems, rewards and sanctions, bullying, sexism and racism
- How data is to be collected in relation to the policy e.g. questionnaires, interviews, observation, reports and monitoring forms
- A current behavioural baseline that enables the institution to evaluate the effect of the policy on behaviour
- Whether to involve an outside consultant to assist with various aspects of developing a policy

Decision-making and data-collection methods:

There are various data-collection methods that can be used:

- Surveys of staff and pupil opinion on e.g. incidence and prevalence of specific behaviours and the behaviour policy, using structured or unstructured questionnaires. These need to include representative samples across the NC years and across staff roles.

- Structured interviews can be used to gather in depth information from staff and pupils.

- Observation can be undertaken through pupil shadowing. A sample of pupils is taken from across the NC years and different types of pupils e.g. high /low achievers and the well-behaved and disruptive.

  The pupil is followed from lesson to lesson over a whole day which enables the observer to gather information as to how the pupil behaves in different contexts and with different staff.

- Collecting statistics kept on referrals and sanctions.

Where there is a documented referral process it is possible to gain some idea as to:

- The incidence and prevalence of specific behaviour problems
- The kinds of pupils involved
- The pupils who reoffend
- The staff involved

The school council can be used as a means of gathering pupil opinion on behaviour in the school and strategies for promoting positive behaviour

One should be aware of practicalities involved in data collection:

- The time and effort required.
- Confidentiality is absolutely necessary given the conflicts that arise among staff over behavioural strategies.

These issues are further discussed in the chapter on assessment.

ORGANIZATIONAL PROBLEMS

Continuity and discontinuity

The WSBP WP may at times experience discontinuities in the the form of unexpected and unpredictable extraneous events or through changes in the composition of the WP. These changes may be destabilising in the sense of causing the WP to lose its sense of direction, its coherence and cohesiveness. On the other hand new staff may bring fresh ideas and renewed vigour to the WP. It would appear essential for a core of staff to continue in order to avoid the negative effects of discontinuity.

Consensus and dissent

It is important for the WSBP to achieve a consensus on the policy. For this to happen it is necessary for the WP to be representative of the staff as a whole and for the Elton Report and relevant DFE circulars to provide the parameters for discussion. Conflicts for example may arise over the use of rewards and sanctions in order to encourage positive behaviour. Reference to Elton may help to forestall this kind of conflict.

Motivation and commitment

It is important that staff are motivated and committed to the WSBP WP and are not members because of inertia or having been 'volunteered'. If staff are apathetic then the WP will suffer from poor attendance and a lack of momentum. Motivation can be highly dependent on the WP being chaired effectively by someone who prepares agendas and circulates necessary documentation (such as minutes prior to the WP meeting) to WP members.

Links with staff

It is necessary to maintain close links with the whole staff in order for there to be ownership of the policy. This can be achieved through:

- Designated INSET days
- Circulation of minutes, proposals and drafts
- Reports in the bulletin
- Questionnaires
- WP members discussing the policy with other members of staff through HOYs / HODs meetings

ROLE OF AN OUTSIDE CONSULTANT

A school may feel it useful to involve an outside consultant. This can arise where the school feels that they need additional expertise or where they have insufficient time to develop some aspects of the policy.

An outside consultant can:

- Bring alternative perspectives to the WP
- Disseminate research and policies and practices from other schools
- Undertake surveys
- Design questionnaires
- Conduct in-depth interviews
- Provide an analysis of data collected

- Provide a more objective and neutral viewpoint and provide an element of confidentiality in feeding back information arising from questionnaires and interviews

- Comment on the discussions, processes and procedures of the WP

DIFFICULTIES OF DEVELOPING POLICY AND PRACTICE IN THE SECONDARY SCHOOL

Difficulties in contextualising the policy

A WSBP should be developed in relation to the particular ethos and context of the school. This may present difficulties for example in terms of the pre-existing approach towards behaviour problems. For instance, there may exist a coercive-punitive ethos in the school which might be in conflict with an Elton-based approach that supports the use of rewards in encouraging positive behaviour.

Difficulties arising from the scale of the institution

The size of the institution in terms of the numbers of staff and pupils might present difficulties. The achievement of staff consistency in dealing with behaviour may prove more difficult with larger numbers of staff and there is greater possibility for disagreement and the emergence of factions.

These difficulties require flexibility in implementing the policy. It is unlikely as well as unnecessary for there to be absolute consistency in dealing with behaviour as long as there is an *agreed range* of actions in relation to behaviour problems. Staff should consistently deal with behaviour problems by drawing from the appropriate range of actions.

Where factions exist it is necessary to ensure that they are represented within the WSBP WP. The Elton Report and DFE circulars can be referred to as a means of arbitrating between conflicting staff perspectives.

Difficulties relating to readiness for organizational change

There are a number of factors that can affect organizational change and which can impede the development of a WSBP:

- A low level of staff morale – a climate of cynicism and pessimism

- Poor communications between SMT and staff

- Inadequate staff cohesiveness – factional conflicts over discipline

- Insufficient or absence of SMT leadership

- Frequent staffing changes – staff turnover

Dissent and conflict re: approaches to behaviour

In a school there may be different viewpoints with regard to the:

- definition of behaviour difficulty
- the incidence and prevalence of misbehaviour
- the causes of behaviour difficulties
- ways of dealing with behaviour difficulties

Staff may differ over what is a behaviour difficulty, they may disagree as to the extent and severity of misbehaviour in the school, they may locate the cause of behaviour problems differently and espouse different strategies for dealing with those problems.

EXAMPLES

Staff may disagree over the enforcement of uniform.

Staff may differ as to whether discipline has deteriorated in the school depending on their perceptions and historical memory. Bias may affect perceptions and memory.

Staff frequently emphasize particular causes for behaviour problems, these causes reflecting a favoured perspective. Staff often subscribe to:

a child-deficit model e.g. a pupil's behaviour difficulty being the result of some skill or quality the pupil inherently lacks.

or

a home-background model e.g. a pupil's difficulty occurs because of poor parenting or family background.

Staff rather infrequently hold:

a teacher-deficit model e.g seeing that the pupil's difficulty may be a result of their lack of effective classroom or behaviour management.

or

an interactionist model e.g. seeing the pupil's difficulty as resulting from an interaction between teacher and pupil or school and pupil.

Public consensus / Private dissent in policy and practice

Staff may publicly agree with a WSBP but in private entertain doubts about the principles underlying the WSBP and its effectiveness in changing pupils' behaviour. Unless the policy is supported by the staff it will be ineffective. Staff should have opportunities to express their opinions anonymously so that dissenting views can be discussed. A true consensus of staff opinion should then emerge once those views have been satisfactorily addressed.

Data collection difficulties

A number of difficulties may present themselves when collecting data:

- The data required may not exist or if existing may not cover the period or take the form required
- There may not be the time available to collect data covering all staff or all pupils. This may lead to problems regarding the representativeness of the sample
- When collected, the data may be open to different interpretations
- The data collected may be sensitive, particularly with regard to staff, and its use therefore may be circumscribed

Consultation difficulties

When a school makes use of a consultant, a number of difficulties can present themselves:

- Maintaining neutrality and objectivity
- Deciding how consultation will be arranged
- Deciding how high one's profile should be in the school and WP
- Discontinuities in terms of processes and procedures
- Negative climate for change

Implementation

Implementation should be considered in terms of:

- a realistic time frame that accepts that change in a large institution is slow and that too quick a pace is likely to foster resistance and end in failure
- any time constraints currently operating e.g. in terms of meetings and other demands on staff time
- staff attitudes towards implementation e.g. pessimism and inertia may affect the willingness of staff to implement the policy or they may feel unable to implement it due to lack of time or the necessary skills

'Paper Policies'

A WSBP may take the form of a 'paper policy' i.e. a policy that has been formulated by the SMT without whole staff involvement and ownership. A 'paper policy' will be difficult to implement and will fail to achieve effective change.

Difficulties in involving the wider community

It is desirable to involve the wider community particularly parents and carers in formulating the policy. This can prove difficult if it is thought necessary to contact a representative sample of parents and carers. Meetings can be arranged but sparsely attended. Questionnaires can be posted but returns may be low. Involvement of parent-governors may often be the best solution.

Difficulties in evaluating change

Evaluation of the policy requires the detection of positive behavioural change in the school.

A pre-implementation baseline has to be established so comparisons can be made between the *school as it was* and *how it is after the policy* has had sufficient time to work.

The evaluation of the policy will depend on the performance indicators selected and what level of performance is thought achievable over a realistic time-frame.

Performance indicators can be:

- exclusion rate
- detention rate
- rate of referrals to HOYs / tutors
- rate of referrals to a referral room
- amount of vandalism

Schools can have performance indicators based on positive behaviour:

- number of pupils who have received Merit Marks
- number of pupils who have positive letters sent to parents / carers
- numbers of pupils who have cooperated by reporting incidents of bullying

Use of such indicators will depend on the reliability of school records in terms of accuracy and consistency of usage.

Schools will need to consider what counts as success in terms of the implementation of the policy. This means finding out what changes, if any, have occurred with regard to particular types of behaviour. Additionally it is necessary to consider whether these reductions are significant and attributable to the WSBP.

There is a possibility that behavioural change may be the result of factors other than the WSBP e.g.

- changes in the reliability and accuracy of school records
- staff changes / turnover
- changes in school population
- yearly intake differences
- curriculum changes

The above points need to be considered when finally coming to a decision about the effectiveness of the WSBP.

---

8. MONITORING AND EVALUATING A BEHAVIOUR POLICY

WHY EVALUATE?

Evaluation of school policies is often neglected or treated as an afterthought. Given the overwhelming pressure on time and resources, teachers, and others involved in the process of developing and implementing policy, are eager to move on to the next task. Many teachers feel that they do not have the knowledge or skills to evaluate, and others feel concerned that evaluation might highlight deficiencies in their work or devalue their efforts.

However, to neglect evaluation for any of these reasons would be a mistake. Whole school policy development is not, or should not be, a one off event but an ongoing cycle of change and review. Evaluation has an important contribution to make in this cycle. It enables schools to look objectively at what has been achieved, what works well, and why. At the same time it enables them to identify what is not working, what needs to be improved or modified in response to a changing environment. Evaluation is essentially about asking the right questions. What these questions might be, and appropriate ways of asking them are the subjects of this chapter.

WHAT TO EVALUATE?

Progress in Relation to Intended Outcomes

Evaluation needs to be considered from the very outset of policy development, in the sense that a school or working party needs to have developed a vision of the outcomes they are aiming to achieve. It is in relation to this vision that an evaluation will be made.

Defining success criteria enables schools to identify the specific kinds of information they will need to collect prior to the implementation of a policy (baselines) and at various points during implementation (performance criteria) in order to evaluate the success of their policy.

Unintended Outcomes

What else has changed during the course of this project that was not intended, or anticipated? Let us call it serendipity. Teachers working in a school which set out to address particular problems in the lunchtime break, noticed after implementation of a playground policy, that classroom behaviour during the afternoon was much improved. Children settled more quickly to their work, and time that was previously taken up settling scores from the lunchtime break was used far more productively

The Process

Many schools will be interested, not only in collecting information about the outcome of their work, but also about the processes that they used. For example, one headteacher, in discussing the impact of policy development in her school, noted that teachers in the school were now able to go along with majority decisions and support them, even when these differed from their own views. She said staff had learned to trust each other, and this was reflected in other areas of school life.

What Does It Mean?

Evaluating changes in any real life situation, especially a situation as complex as a school, is not a straightforward business. Schools are not scientific laboratories, and it is never possible to say with absolute certainty, 'This change in policy has resulted in this change in behaviour or attitude'. Many factors affect the way pupils and teachers behave, what they think, and how they feel. However, this should never be used as a reason not to collect evaluative information.

In analysing information, those working within a school setting can weigh up the significance of various factors, and make reasonable inferences about the impact of whole school policy and procedures on any changes that have occurred.

A staff group in one secondary school worked very hard to establish a clear procedure for beginning lessons. They found that this seemed to pay off in terms of improved behaviour, less noise, and more completed work. Another factor which contributed to this outcome was the amalgamation of the school which was previously on two sites some ten minutes walk from each other.

We shall return to the issue of analysis further on in this chapter. First we will discuss ways in which evaluative information can be collected.

How to evaluate

Evaluation relies on monitoring, or collecting information by various means. The methods that are used will depend upon what is being evaluated. There are a number of common issues to be considered in any method of information gathering. These are:

- **Validity:** The information collected must represent as accurately as possible those issues which are being evaluated and not be confounded with other issues

- **Reliability:** The information must constitute a reliable and representative sample, and not be biased in terms of where or when it is collected, or who is doing the collecting.

- **Confidentiality:** All information must be held confidentially, and not be publicized in a way which compromises the privacy of individuals or groups.

- **Ease and Economy:** Information must be collected in a way which is as easy and economical as possible in terms of time and resources, not to mention goodwill.

Evaluating Outcomes

In any evaluation of outcomes, baseline information is essential. It is important to have a clear idea of the starting point, in order to measure progress following implementation of a behaviour policy. This is much easier to say than to do, partly because baseline information, by definition, should be collected early on in a project, when people are just beginning to become engaged. Schools record some baseline information anyway, for example records of attendance, exclusions, official punishments, detentions, letters to parents. Other information, for example, incidents of name calling are rarely reported much less recorded, and schools must think quite hard about getting information about these kinds of areas.

Methods of collecting information

Direct observation. One of the simplest methods of collecting information about the occurrence of specific behaviour, either positive or negative, is by direct observation. Such observation may well form part of the assessment process which has been discussed previously in this book. It would be carried out before and after the implementation of policy. Usually a count of the frequency of behaviours is sufficient, but for some types of behaviour for example 'arguing with teachers' measurements of severity or duration may also be significant.

Observations may be made by an individual focusing for a specified period on one or more clearly defined behaviours. Or, they may be made by a number of individuals, who incorporate the recording of incidents of specific behaviour into their ongoing work.

One group of teachers were interested in evaluating the effect of an agreed procedure for getting help from the teacher. They had introduced this procedure to overcome the problem of shouting out. For three days they kept an observation sheet (below) on their desks to record occurrences of shouting out, as well as occurrences of pupils putting up their hand, and after a nod from the teacher, waiting for him/her to come.

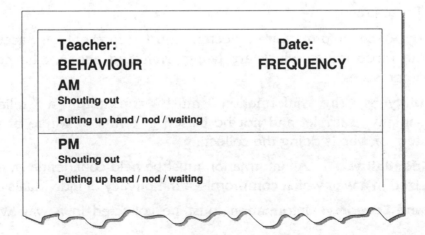

Teacher:	Date:
BEHAVIOUR	**FREQUENCY**
AM	
Shouting out	
Putting up hand / nod / waiting	
PM	
Shouting out	
Putting up hand / nod / waiting	

When the results were compared to similar observations made two terms earlier it was found that not only were there almost no occurrences of shouting out, but that requests for help of any kind were far fewer.

Incident reports. Many negative behaviours are not open to direct observation, at least not by teachers. Bullying is an example of a behaviour which by its very

---

INCIDENTS of BULLYING

What happened?

Where did it happen?

When did it happen?

Date: Time:

Thank you for your help in reporting this incident of bullying

---

nature is hidden. However, given a guarantee of confidentiality pupils will often be prepared to report incidents. In one of our schools a 'bully box' was set up in the school library for one week and all pupils in years 7 & 8 were given Incident Slips to record the nature, time, and place of incidents of bullying which they observed during a one week period. The procedure and purpose were explained in the year group assemblies.

During the week twenty slips were returned. The incidents they describe include 'dirty looks'; 'saying or writing bad things about someone else'; 'forcing someone to take the blame for something'. They occurred primarily in the playground during lunchtime but also in the classroom and outside school. The school developed a new policy on behaviour in the playground and when the study was repeated, some months later, bullying had all but disappeared.

In many cases the recording of serious incidents may be part of a schools existing programme of discipline or may be established as part of the policy on behaviour. Incident reports can be retained and used as the basis for monitoring and evaluation of changing patterns of behaviour, and can also provide a record of whether agreed procedures are actually being used.

The Incident Report on the next page was designed by a nursery school, and used by all staff to create a permanent record of behaviour which they considered unacceptable. At the same time they were encouraged to record instances of children behaving in ways which reflected their overall aim of encouraging independent social skills in their children.

Referral slips for exclusion from lessons, provide a useful source of evaluative

---

information about the occurrence of various forms of behaviour, and the implementation of agreed procedures. It is essential that incident or referral forms are designed in such a way that:

- relevant and accurate information is recorded as simply as possible
- someone hangs on to them
- from time to time someone collates and analyses the results.

INCIDENT REPORT   Date:

Child or children

Area of the Nursery

Please tick the behaviour that best describes what you saw

UNACCEPTABLE BEHAVIOUR

Tantrum – swearing, screaming, throwing themselves about

Verbal aggression – taunting, teasing, name-calling, unkind words

Unprovoked physical aggression – hitting, pushing without apparent reason

Provoked physical aggression – in response to being pushed, teased, hit

Deliberate disobediance – refusing to comply with requests after second request

DESIRABLE BEHAVIOUR

Sharing without adult prompting

Negotiation without adult prompting

Tidying up without adult prompting

Helping another child without adult prompting

Saying sorry (or making amends in another way) without adult prompting

Anything else (please specify)

Staff member recording incident

One secondary school had for some years had a referral slip for teachers to refer pupils out of lessons for unacceptable behaviour. On the face of it, the slip provided a clear format for recording incidents occurring in the classroom to a senior member of staff.

It also provided a format for action taken by the senior staff to be fed back to the class teacher. At the outset of the project the slip was rarely used by teachers, and when it was used they almost never received written feedback on action taken. What they occasionally received was a deputy head storming into the middle of their lesson to berate them in front their pupils for failing to manage behaviour.

In developing policy the senior staff agreed that in managing classroom behaviour, teachers had to know that their authority would be supported and not undermined. A hierarchy of responses to incidents was agreed and implemented. The identical referral slip was retained, and monitoring over a period of one year showed a marked increase in the first two terms of referral slips being used. This gradually fell off during the remaining term. In interpreting this information staff recognised that an initial increase in the rate of referral was a good thing. It reflected a change in relationships between staff and senior managers that was very important for standards of discipline throughout the school.

STUDENT SURVEY   Date:

In your opinion HOW OFTEN do the following behaviours occur in your lessons:

0 = Never   1 = Sometimes   2 = Frequently   3 = Most of the time

a) Swearing at students?	0 1 2 3
b) Swearing at teachers?	0 1 2 3
c) Threatening students?	0 1 2 3
d) Teasing students?	0 1 2 3
e) Shouting out?	0 1 2 3
f) Leaving the classroom without permission	0 1 2 3
g) Making silly noises	0 1 2 3
h) Spoiling other people's work	0 1 2 3
i) Talking quietly about work	0 1 2 3
j) Asking for help from the teacher by putting up hand	0 1 2 3
k) Helping others with their work	0 1 2 3
l) Finishing the work set for the lesson	0 1 2 3
m) Handing in homework on time	0 1 2 3
o) Saying something nice about another person	0 1 2 3

Recording success

On the positive side, records of awards, privileges, merit marks, certificates of achievement, and other forms of rewarding and acknowledging positive behaviour can also be a rich source of evaluative information. Again, it is essential that relevant information related to such behaviour is recorded simply and accurately and that somebody hangs on to it. As such information is collated and analysed it can provide an indicator of how successful the policy is in improving behaviour and achievement in school. Clearly such data must be interpreted carefully. Are we seeing the notorious Hawthorne effect? Is behaviour really better or have we just started noticing better behaviour more often? Does it matter? Research on effectiveness in behaviour support indicates that the perception of positive change in a school or classroom is at least as important as objective change.

Questionnaires are useful in exploring changes in behavioural and non-behavioural issues, for example pupils' attitudes toward school, or staff or parental satisfaction about disciplinary procedures. Used as a tool for evaluation, it is important to collect both 'before' and 'after' questionnaires.

On the face of it questionnaires may seem like a simple way of collecting lots of information from many people without too much effort. This is only true if the questionnaire is well designed, so that questions are unambiguous, clear and easy to answer. It is also important that responses are given in a form that is easy to collate and analyse. Multiple choice or rating scales are particularly useful in this respect, though obviously they limit the 'richness' of information obtained. Pupils are marvellous at collating information - by Key Stage 2 they have learned to tally, are usually quite accurate, and love doing it. A reminder, about confidentiality. Whoever is collating or analysing questionnaires, it is best to ask respondents not to put their names on questionnaires. It is also very useful, and can save time in the long run, to test out questionnaires on a small group of 'typical' respondents, to 'get the kinks out' before distributing them widely.

Interview, Discussion

Interviews can provide very rich information about a range of issues but they are very time consuming. Obviously interviews or discussions in groups are more economical than with individuals, but the limitation here is on what people will reveal in the group situation. The other limitation is on recording and analysing the information discussed. A well structured interview guided by a schedule of questions with space for summary responses is helpful here. Small groups can record their own responses or conclusions and again, providing a format (prepared flip charts) for doing so is a big help.

Documentary Information

As mentioned above, it is possible to tap into documentary information on attendance, and academic achievement, which are collected and available as a matter of public record anyway. These indicators can provide very good evaluative information for schools who are aiming for improved attendance and attainment as a spin-off of improved behaviour. It is important that information is collected in a consistent way.

Many schools and authorities are beginning to develop methods of measuring achievement using the 'value-added' concept and this will obviously provide a useful addition to the information provided by raw SAT's results.

What else to evaluate?

Processes

Many schools will be interested to evaluate not only the outcome of their work, but also the processes which they used to achieve those outcomes. So for example one school held it as a very high priority that at each stage of the work, the fullest possible consultation of staff, pupils and parents was carried out. For our own project team, whose task it was to facilitate the development of policy in project schools, there was also a concern to evaluate the processes used. At the outset of the project we defined the model of our work, the RAFIE model. The stages of this model are reflected in this book. In addition to evaluating various outcomes of this work we were also interested in evaluating the effectiveness of this model.

Using tools like a force field analysis to identify those factors that moved the work forward, and those which hindered progress can be useful. An example of a force field analysis taken from one of our case studies is shown on the next page. As a cumulative record this can be a very useful management tool for future school development.

Force Field Analysis

Facilitating factors:

Opportunity for free training programme for mid-day supervisors

Willingness of staff to trial new systems and pro-formas

Willingness of staff to explore new mechanisms for rewarding pupils

Constraining factors:

Staff perception of time needed to complete new pro-formas

Introduction of two systems of recording at the same time

New pro-forma looks overwhelming for non-teaching staff

Balance:

Full discussion in staff meeting set timetable for introduction of new procedures. Also allayed anxieties about time commitment and follow up.

What else?

Let us not forget the serendipity, the unintended outcome, those changes in the way people behave and feel in an school, changes not necessarily in what people do, but in how they do it.

For example relationships between staff have moved onto a different footing as a result of working together on a team. Parents and governors are now more often coming into school and helping out in the classroom. Pupils formed a school council as a result of their work on the behaviour policy.

What else has changed during the course of this project that was not intended, or anticipated? Whatever methods of evaluative research are being used, it is always worth including open ended questions, such as those below. These were written as part of an evaluation interview with head teachers whose schools had been involved with behaviour policy projects.

- Are there any changes in behaviour which have come about as a result of this project?

- Can you describe your general impression of the project and its impact on your school?

- Are there any other changes either positive or negative which you had not anticipated?

Analysing the results

As suggested above, it is never possible in the real life situation to establish a scientifically verifiable cause and effect relationship between the development and implementation of policy and any observed change in behaviour or attitude. However it is certainly possible for those working within a given school to make reasonable inferences about this relationship, and the impact of other factors.

Analysing evaluative information is not a task for one or two individuals in a school, but a task for a group or perhaps a whole staff meeting or INSET. It is certainly helpful to have available a clear summary of the information collected on both outcomes and process. But analysis is a very important thinking task and the more ideas and perspectives that are brought to bear, the more fruitful the result. There are several questions that then need to be asked:

- *Which of the original objectives and success criteria have been met?*

- *If objectives have been met, why have they?*

- *What aspects of the policy have been helpful?*

- *What else has been helpful or contributed to our success?*

- *If objectives have not been met, why haven't they?*

- *What aspects of the policy have not been so helpful?*

- *What else has stopped us going forward or achieving success?*

- *What else has been achieved (or lost) in this process which was not anticipated?*

The answers to these questions lead on to the next and most important question:

What do we need to do next?

In the light of the analysis, which aspects of the policy need to be retained expanded, or strengthened? What needs to be added or changed? What needs to be done next to maintain the gains that have been made or generalize them to other areas. Does the analysis point to problems which had not been identified previously? Are there factors limiting progress which had not been considered in the original assessment? Are particular procedures increasing difficulties or creating new difficulties, or simply not being used because they are unworkable. How can they be adapted or streamlined to make them more useful. What can be learned about the actual process of policy development which can be applied to other aspects of development within the school? What needs to happen next.

It can be seen that within this approach to evaluation, one is not concerned so much with success and failure as such, but with learning and going forward from experience.

9. INVOLVING SENIOR COLLEAGUES

The need for clear definitions of roles

A critical moment in putting into practice is the point at which a class teacher wishes to involve a more senior member of staff. Repeated problems with a pupil during lessons may cause a teacher to pass the problem up.

What is the more senior teacher's role here? If it is not clearly defined this process can lead to disappointment, anger and resentment. It can sometimes sound and feel like a complaint is being directed at the senior colleague. There can be the unspoken:

> *'You're the senior teacher, it's your job, you have the big guns. You should sort this out.'*

Similarly, the same member of staff who 'passed the problem up' might be expected to deal with a 'complaint' about a pupil from a lunchtime supervisor. The roles are now reversed but the teacher might feel:

> *'You're the one on the spot at lunchtime, how can I be expected to do anything from this remove? This is petty stuff – you should be able to sort it out yourself.'*

Whatever role one finds oneself in, it can be difficult to see the situation from the other person's point of view.

What can be expected to happen when a pupil is referred upwards?

The more senior member of staff will want to be assured that an agreed set of class-based sanctions have been implemented. They should not be expected to immediately takeover responsibility for the problem.

The staff member might accept this provided that they were assured that they would:

- **not be left alone** to work out the strategies for solving the problem

- **be supported** in their use of classroom sanction, for example: back-up the teacher when a pupil fails to turn up for a detention.

The 'Oversight' role

Initially, the more senior teacher's role should involve **oversight** of an agreement between the pupil and the staff member, for instance that certain changes occur in the pupil's behaviour in the next lesson.

The staff member, for his/her part, may make a commitment to support the proposed change in the pupil's behaviour in some positive way – for instance, using a low-key reminder of the target behaviour at the appropriate time rather than coming in 'heavy'.

At what point are the big guns employed?

The answer is: that sanctions should be signalled and then used in a gradual and hierarchical order. Moving up the hierarchy should only occur:

- *If clear and reasonable requests have been made of the pupil*
- *If the referring staff-member gives support to the pupil in carrying out these requests*
- *If lower order sanctions have been applied (see Chapter 2)*
- *If an indication has been made to the pupil of what the next step will be should the required change not occur*

Key procedures that support the 'oversight' role
Continue lower order sanctions

Sanctions should be hierarchical but they should also be cumulative. Lower order sanctions should be continued whilst the pupil moves up the hierarchy. Many pupils find that lower order sanctions can cause them more inconvenience than those the school uses later. Lower order sanctions might include: completing work unfinished during a lesson / filling out an incident form / short detention.

Non-compliance with lower order sanctions

In the situation of non-compliance, the following issues should be considered:

- *Non-compliance with a lower order sanction should **never** be a reason for abandoning it*
- *If the pupil does not comply with the sanction (eg not turning up for a detention) then the **hierarchical measures should be applied until there are behaviour changes***
- ***The certainty of the matter being pursued** is likely to be more powerful in the pupil's eyes than quickly employing 'the big guns'. (See page 11)*
- ***Defiance of the school's procedures is more serious than the pupil's original actions***

Staff 'anger' and the oversight role

Schools might find it valuable to agree on a statement about the appropriate communication of anger towards pupils. This might be an agreement that anger, by itself, is **not** a sanction, but that it is likely to represent only a warning of further action. For the pupil, it can indicate **a temporary withdrawal** or reversal of existing interpersonal rewards stemming from a good relationship. If such a relationship has not been established, the staff member's discomfort (their anger) may well be **more** rewarding for the pupil than the avoidance of an impending sanction. This is especially true if the pupil thinks that the staff member either does not have the determination to use a sanction or has none available.

Pupil anger

It should be agreed in the statements of roles that a pupil being angry is not in itself a sanctionable behaviour. It is the behaviour which might result from the pupil's feelings which is of concern. If staff over-react – show too much anger, it can:

- make it difficult for the senior member of staff to effectively perform their 'oversight' role as part of a hierarchy of sanctions
- make it less likely that any parental involvement will be supportive

INVOLVING SENIOR COLLEAGUES

The following questions are important for staff to consider:

At what point should a more senior member of staff be involved?

What level of behaviour, either in terms of severity or frequency, will trigger involvement?

Will the 'critical level' be determined by individual teacher's level of tolerance or will the staff (perhaps departments in a secondary school) agree more objective criteria?

What can classroom teachers expect from more senior colleagues if they become involved?

What can senior staff expect from classroom teachers if they become involved?

How will new or temporary members of staff find out about these procedures?

Will there be a separate procedure for involving senior staff in a 'crisis' as opposed to dealing with repeated low-level behaviour?

BIBLIOGRAPHY

Ainscow, M., Hopkins, D., Southworth, G., West, M., (1995) *Creating the Conditions for School Improvement.* London: David Fulton Publishers

Ayers, H., Clarke, D., and Ross, A., (1996) *Assessing Individual Needs: A Practical Approach.* 2nd Edition. London: David Fulton Publishers

Ayers, H., Clarke, D., Murray, A., (1995) *Perspectives on Behaviour.* London: David Fulton Publishers

DFE, (1994) *Pupils with Problems.* London: HMSO

Daniels, H. and Corrie, L., (1993) The Management of Discipline in Special Schools in *The Management of Behaviour in Schools,* Varma, V., (Editor). London: Longman

Dreikurs, Rudolf, (1982) *Maintaining Sanity in the Classroom,* New York: Harper Collins

Fisher, R., and Ury, W., (1987) *Getting to Yes,* London: Arrow Business Books

Greenhalgh, Paul, (1994) *Emotional Growth and Learning.* London: Routledge

Lawrence, D., (1988) *Enhancing Self-esteem in the Classroom,* London: Paul Chapman Publishing Ltd

Ofsted (1993), *Achieving Good Behaviour in Schools,* London: HMSO

Oppenheim, A.N. (1993), *Questionnaire Design, Interviewing and Attitude Measurement.* London: Pinter publishers

Robertson, John, (1989) (Second Edition) *Effective Classroom Control.* London: Hodder & Stoughton

Rogers, Bill, (1994) *Behaviour Recovery.* Melbourne: ACER

Rogers, Bill, (1990) *You Know the Fair Rule.* Harlow: Longman

Rogers, Bill, (1994) *The Language of Discipline.* Plymouth: Northcote House Publishers

Rogers, Bill, (1992) *Supporting Teachers in the Workplace.* Queensland: Jacaranda Press

Videos

Rogers, Bill, (1994 – 5), *Prevention, Positive Correction, Consequences, Repair and Rebuild.* London: Quartus Pty Ltd

Managing Behaviour in Secondary Schools, Strathclyde LEA

MATERIALS AND EXAMPLES

Policy issues and examples

Gathering Information

100 – 101   Classroom Discipline Questionnaire
An example of a broad approach to information gathering, requiring answers to fairly open questions

102   Classroom Behaviours Questionnaire
Example of a questionnaire using closed questions to gather information about specific practice using continua for responses.

103   Positive Strategies Questionnaire
A mostly closed set of questions, but this time requiring underlining as a means of response.

Whole School Strategies

104   3 Step technique for conflict resolution in the primary school.

105   Incident / Record Form
This form could be used where there were agreed school-wide rules and where pupils were being encouraged to take responsibility for their own behaviour. In at least one school using such a form, few referrals are accepted by the headteacher without the pupil having filled one in. This kind of information can also be very useful in determining whether a pupil should be included in the SEN register.

106 – 107   A primary induction booklet for 'casual entrants'.
This is particularly useful for children who enter during the year and who miss the standard class induction programme. These children seem to be frequently highly represented when sanctions are monitored. Translation into home languages would be a powerful way of integrating new pupils who have very little English.

Policy development activities

108   Activities to promote reflection and discussion on behavioural issues
These are aimed at the Primary level, but they would be easy to adapt for use in a PHSE lesson in a secondary school

109   Two activities about feelings
Two activities for staff to do which explore the feelings involved in behaviour management

110 – 111   Activity for developing positive rules with secondary students

112   Staff activity – This sheet provides the basis for staff to identify the behaviours that cause concern in a school and also to reach a consensus as to how serious they are.

POLICY AND PRACTICE *AIDE MEMOIRE*

What are the school's aims?

What are the values that the school holds?

How do you want pupils to behave? What school rules exist?
Do they cover safety and movement / Getting teacher's attention / Treatment of each other / How to sort out problems

How does the school encourage and acknowledge appropriate behaviour?
At a class level?   Departmental level?   At an organisational level?
Are they formal or informal?   Through the curriculum?
Through employing routines that avoid difficulties and conflicts?
Through providing opportunities to give pupils choice / responsibilities?   Through raising self-esteem?   Through providing positive feedback?
Through the use of clear and consistent procedures?
Through having clear boundaries, predictably reinforced?
Through addressing the 'affective' curriculum

Do staff agree about how serious different behaviours are?
Trivial / Moderately Serious / Very Serious?

How do class teachers / the school respond to misbehaviour at these different levels? In particular how do teachers respond to repeated instances of misbehaviour? What range of preferred responses are available

How do more senior colleagues become involved? What is the nature of their involvement?

Are there clear guidelines for when and how classroom teachers should involve more senior members of staff?

Are there agreed emergency procedures for the removal of a pupil from a classroom?

Are there clear procedures for dealing with particular areas of concern eg violence, sexual harassment, racism, bullying?

Are there clear procedures and practice for dealing with behaviour in: playground, corridors, trips, assemblies, lunchtimes?

How much have pupils / parents / governors been involved in the development of the policy? Does this need to change?

How is the effectiveness of the policy monitored and evaluated?

How does the Behaviour Policy link with other policies eg EO / SEN?

from **Developing and Implementing a Whole-School Behaviour Policy**   eds. D. Clarke and A. Murray

Timetable for Developing A Behaviour Policy

Task	Task Group	Completion Date
Gather information – Observations / surveys	**Working Party**	_____
Staff discussion – *What makes children behave well?* – *Why do children misbehave?*	**Staff**	_____
Defining the Problem and laying out the task	**Staff and Governors**	_____
'Staff Responsibilities'	**Working Party**	_____
Individual staff for approval		
Work with Children	**Staff and pupils**	_____
'Pupil Responsibilities'	**Pupils**	_____
1st Draft **'How we encourage Good Behaviour'** **'What we do when pupils misbehave'**	**All Staff and Working Party**	_____
To all staff for written comments	**Staff**	_____
2nd Draft	**Working Party**	_____
To Governors for comments	**Governors**	_____
3rd Draft	**Working Party**	_____
Parents' Meeting	**Parents**	_____
Full Staff Meeting for approval	**Full staff**	_____
'Parent Responsibilities' **Governors**	**Chair**	_____
Collation of all sections of Policy to form.....	**Working Party**	_____
..... the Implementation Draft	**Full staff**	_____
Final Arrangements for Implementation	**Whole School**	_____

Designed by Alastair Ross

from **Developing and Implementing a Whole-School Behaviour Policy**   eds. D. Clarke and A. Murray

Behaviour Policy Development Checklist 1

	Policy	Handbook	How? Who?	Start Date	Completion Date
Aims and Values	Link the broad aims of the school to behaviour. Include Aims and Values from school brochure.				
Rights	Identify the rights of different members of the school community based upon the values held by the school.	Detail the rights of different members with examples.			
Responsibilities	Briefly indicate different groups' responsibilities	Detail teachers' responsibilities in implementing the behaviour policy			
Define acceptable behaviour	Indicate the kind of behaviour expected from pupils. Broadly define the rules with examples. These might be expressed in terms of Rights and Responsibilities.	Detail appropriate behaviour			
Define unacceptable behaviour	Briefly describe unacceptable behaviour. Indicate that serious misbehaviour includes repeated instances of minor misbehaviour.	Detail the range of misbehaviour from minor through to very serious. Define what behaviours warrant removal from class and exclusion.			
Describe how the school encourages appropriate behaviour	Outline how the school encourages appropriate behaviour. This would include: what the school does by way of PRO-ACTIVE and RESPONSIVE strategies.	Detail how the school encourages acceptable behaviour including the systems for 'rewarding' effort and achievement.			
Describe the organisation and procedures for responding to unacceptable behaviour	Indicate the range of responses to different kinds of behaviour. Describe how responses should be related to the misbehaviour. Indicate that repeated instances of misbehaviour will be treated as more serious. Indicate that there will be different responses for more or less serious behaviour. Indicate that responses will be fair. Indicate that pupils will be encouraged to take responsibility for their own behaviour.	Detail the systems and procedures for responding to misbehaviour in and out of the classroom. Define different levels of misbehaviour. Define appropriate ranges of response to the different levels. Make clear that responses should be fair, appropriate and related. Make clear different staff's responsibilities; in particular, how senior members of staff become involved. Describe the agreed exit-from-room procedure.			
Monitoring and Evaluation	Indicate that this will happen	Detail how this will happen and what performance indicators will be used and frequency of monitoring.			

Behaviour Policy Development Checklist 2

	What needs to happen	Who	Start date	Completion
Working party sessions				
Staff Meetings				
INSET				
Activities with pupils				
Activities with parents				
Activities with support staff				
Policy development				
Handbook development				
Implementation				

from **Developing and Implementing a Whole-School Behaviour Policy** eds. D. Clarke and A. Murray

Developing a Behaviour Policy

Strengths	Weaknesses

Opportunities	Threats

from **Developing and Implementing a Whole-School Behaviour Policy**   eds. D. Clarke and A. Murray

Things we don't like people doing in the playground

Adults telling you off when you haven't done anything wrong

Fighting - some people come and hit you for no reason

People taking your ball when you're playing football

People running round and bumping in to you

Being laughed at when someone is sad

People hurting you in the toilets

Drinking water and spitting it

Play fighting becoming real

Sticking their tongues out

Some people pull hair

Pushing on the stairs

Cursing your family

Boys hitting girls

Showing fingers

Being rude

Bullying

Teasing

Lying

Teasing

Telling tales

Pulling your chair

Hitting with rulers

Boys not tidying up

People being unkind

Children making noises

Not looking after things

Having to line up for a long time

Tearing books in the book corner

Not paying attention to the teacher

Children hiding other people's things

Messing up my work makes me fed up

The teacher telling you off for nothing

Not having a story because children talking

Somebody knocks you and makes you do your work wrong

Things we don't like people doing in class

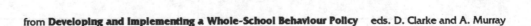

from **Developing and Implementing a Whole-School Behaviour Policy**   eds. D. Clarke and A. Murray

What we do when children misbehave:

'Yellow Card' behaviour

This is behaviour which is not very serious but needs us to ask children to stop

We can do this by:
Reminding them of the playground rule they are breaking
Talking to the child

If they continue to misbehave we may have to remind them again.

'Orange Card' behaviour

'Orange Card' behaviour is more serious misbehaviour, for instance:
a more serious fight
rudeness to playground staff
not stopping 'Yellow Card' behaviour after they have received a warning

What happens:
They have to sit on The Bench for 5 minutes
If they settle down, they can go back and play.
If not, they may have to stay on The Bench or walk round with a member of staff.

'Red Card' behaviour

This is for very serious behaviour or not stopping 'Orange Card' Behaviour. The Senior Meals Supervisor will fill in a 'Red Card Sheet' and give it the class teacher so that they can follow it up. A child who regularly receives a 'Red Card' may be excluded from lunchtimes for a period. This will be discussed with parents

In an emergency

If a child needs to be removed from the playground the Senior Meals Supervisor will send another child to the staffroom with the "EMERGENCY CARD" that she carries as part of her 'PLAYGROUND KIT'.

Concerns

The Senior Meals Supervisor will also let teachers know if she has concerns about a child that has been upset or has found it difficult in the playground.

What we do:

We make sure all of the playground is supervised
We make the rules clear to the children and warn them when necessary
We encourage children to play sensibly and safely

What the children can expect from us:

Make sure they are safe
Treat them with respect at all times, even when they misbehave
Be firm and fair with them
Listen to to them, especially if they are upset or concerned
Notice them when things are not going well for them
Comfort them when they are upset or hurt

There are a two playground rules:
To play sensibly and safely

This means:
No hanging around the toilets
No climbing or going into areas they shouldn't be in
Not pushing people or pulling their clothes
No fighting or playfighting or playing Power Rangers
No spitting

To treat all other people pleasantly and with respect

This means:
Doing what the staff ask
Not spoiling other people's games and helping other children join in your games
Not doing things that might upset or hurt others
Not being cheeky or rude to staff

We can encourage good behaviour by:

Praising pupils when we notice them behaving sensibly (particularly those children who do not find this easy).
Show the children how to play different games
We encourage good behaviour by *'catching them being good'*

Two pages adapted from playground supervisors' handbooks

from Developing and Implementing a Whole-School Behaviour Policy   eds. D. Clarke and A. Murray

West Lodge Primary School

Aims:

To encourage a positive, calm and purposeful atmosphere where pupils can learn to the best of their abilities

To create an atmosphere where all pupils feel valued themselves and treat all others with respect

To encourage children to take responsibility for their their behaviour

To encourage pupils to sort out difficulties in peaceful ways

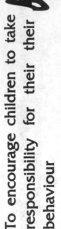

West Lodge
Primary School

Behaviour Policy

from **Developing and Implementing a Whole-School Behaviour Policy** eds. D. Clarke and A. Murray

Rights of Pupils

To be able to learn to the best of their ability

To be treated with consideration and respect

To be listened to by the adults in the school

To know what is expected

To feel safe

To be treated fairly

Rights of Staff

To be treated with respect, by pupils, parents and colleagues

To be able to teach without unnecessary interruption

The Rights of Parents

To be sure their children are treated fairly and with respect

To know that their children are safe

To be able to raise concerns with staff and to be told when there are difficulties

Responsibilities of Pupils

To treat others with consideration and respect

To listen when it is others turn to talk

To follow instructions from teachers and other staff

To sort out difficulties without making matters worse

To ask for help if you need it

To do your best and let others learn

Responsibilities of Staff

To create a safe and stimulating environment in which the pupils can learn

Treating pupils with consistency and respect at all times

Communicating regularly with parents

Responsibilities of Parents

To get our children to school on time, ready to work

To treat other people's children with respect and tell the school staff if you are not satisfied with them

To talk to our children about the things they learn in school

To tell the teachers if our child is being bullied or upset

If you have any questions please see Mr Scotney

Four pages adapted from primary behaviour policies

from **Developing and Implementing a Whole-School Behaviour Policy**   eds. D. Clarke and A. Murray

PUPIL REFERRAL UNIT BEHAVIOUR POLICY

Aims

The aim of these centres is to provide an environment in which young people who have had difficulties in school can:

Access the National Curriculum

Develop their own potential and enable them to make progress

Prepare themselves for full-time education or post-school opportunities

Have the opportunity to develop their social skills

To encourage the development of motivation and self-discipline

Rights and Responsibilities

Everybody has the right to feel safe from physical or verbal threat or attack

Everybody has the right to be able to work and learn without other people making it difficult

Everybody has the right to be treated with fairness and respect at all times

Everybody has the right to have their concerns listened to

Each person has the responsibility to help themselves and others to get the best out of the Centre.

Each Centre has rules which are discussed with pupils which define the behaviour that is expected.

Staff have the responsibility to impose fair consequences on pupils who significantly break these rules.

How we encourage appropriate behaviour

Staff do this by:

- Creating and maintaining a secure, learning environment where pupils can learn free from physical or emotional threat
- Setting and maintaining clear limits and imposing appropriate consequences where necessary
- Encouraging pupils to trust staff through treating pupils fairly and with respect at all times
- Having high expectations of pupils and providing positive feedback about pupils' efforts and achievements
- Setting work that is relevant and appropriate to pupils' abilities
- Making it clear to pupils the way they are expected to behave and not to behave
- When incidents do happen, encouraging pupils to act honestly and to make it clear that they can make it 'all right' either with 'group meetings' or through individual discussions with staff
- Encouraging pupils to discuss their concerns, either individually with staff or as part of a group meeting
- By protecting pupils' legal rights eg under the Children Act
- Ensuring Equal Opportunities are actively maintained
- Informing parents about their children's progress

Example of a behaviour policy used in a Pupil Referral Unit

from **Developing and Implementing a Whole-School Behaviour Policy** eds. D. Clarke and A. Murray

Behaviour we expect

We have general rules which describe the kinds of behaviour we expect:
We expect people in the centres to:

Follow the centre rules and legal requirements
Arrive at the right time and be ready to work and behave sensibly
Do the work that is set and to allow others to do the same
Treat others (other pupils, staff, visitors) with fairness and respect
Act in ways which do not endanger themselves or others
Take responsibility for their own behaviour / learning
Avoid inappropriate behaviour which makes other people uncomfortable

Undesirable behaviour

This is behaviour which is unpleasant or inappropriate. Pupils will be reminded that their behaviour is inappropriate and be requested to stop. If their undesirable behaviour persists then pupils will be warned that their behaviour is becoming unacceptable and will then be treated as more serious.

Undesirable behaviours include:

Offensive behaviour
Behaviour which makes it difficult for other pupils to learn and teachers to teach effectively
Inappropriate use of equipment or mistreatment of the environment
Failure to comply with 'fair consequences' imposed by staff

Unacceptable behaviour

These are behaviours for which exclusion (temporary or permanent) from the premises is likely. They can be regarded as unacceptable because of the severity of a particular behaviour or because of the frequency of less serious behaviour (as described above). Serious behaviours include:

Bullying, racism or sexual harassment   *Endangering others*

Use of illegal substances   *Damage to property*

Pupils should be clear that behaving in these ways can lead to:

Temporary or Permanent exclusion from the centre-based provision

Staff will aim to 'match' the level of their response to the degree of seriousness of the misbehaviour, so that pupils are aware that:

* *their behaviour is being responded to fairly and appropriately*

* *if their misbehaviour is repeated it will be treated with increasing severity*

Monitoring and Evaluation of Policy

The Behaviour Policy will be monitored and regularly reviewed

Discipline

Most discipline will be carried out by positive means. Much conflict can be avoided through appropriate work and comprehensive planning.

Children's names can be recorded in the Good Book for reading out on Fridays. A record of children so recorded should be kept to ensure fairness. Please avoid stereotyping (eg girls always cleaning up).

Positive means of encouragement in individual classrooms or year groups are encouraged, please bear in mind the following points and ask the the Head if in doubt:
- *does your system conflict with or undermine the whole school system?*
- *does your system unintentionally discriminate against individuals or groups?*

All staff have a responsibility for discipline in the school and are expected to deal immediately with any situation they witness.

Each class will decide on the class rules at the beginning of the school year, a copy will be clearly displayed in the classroom and signed by the children.

A child who will not respond to being warned to stop misbehaving should be sent to the paired classroom for a limited time with work. A record should be kept of this, three times in a half term would suggest involving the parents.

Children should never be left to stand outside the classroom as a punishment.

Corporal punishment is not allowed and exposes the teacher to legal action. Physical restraint or 'manhandling' should not be used except in exceptional circumstances. If there is clearly a danger to a child involved then restraint could be used but for as little time as possible and with as little force as possible.

Unintentional assault (eg child scratched as you gestured) or a physical assault caused by a situation getting out of hand should

be reported to the Head immediately. Prompt action in such cases always helps in getting a good resolution to the problem.

Staff should deal quietly and respectfully with children. Shouting should be avoided except in exceptional circumstances.

Children will not usually be disciplined as whole classes.

Children will not be stopped from doing PE or swimming or visits except if offences are related to that subject or to behaviour off-site. If a child has misbehaved off-site they should normally be given the chance to go on the next visit if they can be accompanied at all times by their parent or carer.

Children will not be sent to the Head for bad behaviour except by previous arrangement or when the usual procedures have failed. A senior member of staff should be sent for if a child will not leave the classroom when asked.

Children should be sent to the Head for good behaviour or good work.

Children can be kept in at playtime by their own teacher or in punishment playtime according to the usual procedures.

Children will get a white slip for medium serious (or repeated minor) misdemeanour outside the classroom. They will then stay in at playtime in the hall. Not turning up for your punishment results in two missed playtimes.

Three white slips in a half term will result in a letter home, class teachers are responsible for keeping a record of white slips. If you think a white slip was given in error (either too harsh or too lenient) please consult the Head or Deputy.

All serious misdemeanours (ie premeditated or severe violence, intimidation, swearing at an adult) should always be dealt with by senior staff.

Teachers should consider the potential dangers of disciplining children where there are no witnesses, although this must be balanced against the undoubted advantages of disciplining without an audience of the child's peers.

Two pages on behaviour management from a staff handbook

from **Developing and Implementing a Whole School Behaviour Policy**   eds. D. Clarke and A. Murray

Hierarchy of Sanctions - *recommended practices*

The Look

Hand sign

Rule reminder

Warning 1 2 3

Related sanction eg make up work, clean up mess

Move place (in class timeout)/stand on wall/change or restrict playground

Time out of class/white slip and punishment playtime

Letter home from teacher (3 times out/3 white slips) consider SEN 1 unless clearly temporary (eg new baby, bereavement, new to school)

On report to teacher

Letter home from HT

On report to HT

Formal warning letter from HT

Exclusion one day / Week lunchtime exclusion

Exclusion two day

Exclusion five day (Governors meet)

Permanent exclusion (Governors meeting, LEA involvement)

The decision as to where to start is clearly the art of the process. You need to give yourself enough room to progress at the same time as giving the message to the other children and to the parents that you will not accept the behaviour (everybody makes mistakes about this sometimes. Including me!) The amount of significance that you give to the sanction is clearly important. If you throw missed playtimes around they do not seem very serious; if you make a huge fuss about one minute detentions then fifteen minutes will seem like an enormous punishment.

Children (and adults) often complain that 'nobody did anything' so it is necessary to let victims know what happened. When a child is excluded the class should know this and why (messages about bullying etc can be reinforced at this point). If the class concerned have correct information about an exclusion the message will get around the school. Parents may also need to be informed about what happened to the child that hit, bit etc their child.

Repeated minor misdemeanours should be treated as more serious misdemeanors.

As far as possible children should be able to start afresh after punishment with the clear message that the punishment has settled their debt to the school.

A Hierarchy of Sanctions from a staff handbook

CLASSROOM DISCIPLINE QUESTIONNAIRE

Please indicate what Key Stage you teach

Please write down your classroom rules

How were the rules decided?

How are the pupils made aware of the rules?

What strategies do you use to encourage pupils to comply with the rules?

What consequences do you use when the rules are significantly infringed?

What sort of behaviours do you think warrant removal from the classroom?

---

from **Developing and Implementing a Whole-School Behaviour Policy**   eds. D. Clarke and A. Murray

Give examples of ways in which the school encourages / promotes 'good behaviour'

At an individual level

At the institutional level

Give examples of effective ways in which the school responds to misbehaviour

At an individual level

At the institutional level

Please give other ways in which you consider the school manages behaviour well

What concerns do you have about the way behaviour is managed in the school?

CLASSROOM BEHAVIOURS QUESTIONNAIRE

Key Stage [ ]

Please estimate how often, per day, these behaviours occur, by circling the appropriate number:

0 = Never   1 = Less than once   2 = At least once   3 = Several times   4 = Many times

A)   Task avoidance
Day-dreaming / Fidgetting / Fiddling / Chatting / Wandering about / Disputing instructions

0   1   2   3   4

B)   Interrupting teacher
'Notice me' behaviour / Calling out whilst class teaching / Clowning /
Lateness on arrival / Punctuality after playtime / Moving around on the carpet

0   1   2   3   4

C)   Defiance of authority
Refusal to stop misbehaving or accept reprimand / Swearing at teacher / Answers back
General rudeness / Refusal to work or follow instructions / 'Make me' behaviour
Arguing with teacher / Insolence / Rudeness to non-teaching staff

0   1   2   3   4

D)   Hindering other children working
Squabbling / Interrupting peers / Extended chatting / Calling out to other pupils

0   1   2   3   4

E)   Verbal hostility towards peers
Swearing at peers / Being unkind or hurtful / Teasing / Cussing / Exclusion (you're not my
friend - you can't play with us) / Winding others up / Egging others on / Threats

0   1   2   3   4

F)   Physical hostility towards peers
Poking / Hitting / Tripping / Fighting / Stealing

0   1   2   3   4

G)   Inconsiderate interpersonal behaviour
Running / Pushing / Shoving / Barging in / Grabbing equipment / Being noisy / Interrupting
teacher when talking to other students / Use of swear words

0   1   2   3   4

H)   Inconsiderate use of property / equipment / environment
Damaging other's work / Graffiti / Damaging equipment or environment /Dangerous use of
equipment

0   1   2   3   4

I)   Over-reaction to normal situations
Destroys own work / Sulks / Rudeness / Storms out of room / Hides / Cries / Tantrums

0   1   2   3   4

Please add other classroom behaviours causing concern:

from **Developing and Implementing a Whole-School Behaviour Policy**   eds. D. Clarke and A. Murray

POSITIVE STRATEGIES QUESTIONNAIRE

Key Stage ☐   Where appropriate indicate the frequency

N = Never   O = Occasionally   F = Fairly often   W = What would I do without it?

1)   Have you developed your class rules in conjunction with your students?

Are they on show?

Do you refer to them when dealing with misbehaviour?

2)   What low-level behaviour management strategies do you use?

The Look!	Proximity	Diversions	Refocusing
Simple directions	Rule reminders	Avoiding using the word 'No'	
Non-verbal signals	Giving a choice	Giving a warning of a consequence	
Take-up Time	In-class Time Out	Out-of-class Time Out	

Others:

3)   What positive strategies do you use?

Non-verbal approval	Verbal approval / acknowledgement	
Smiley faces	Wall chart for positive behaviours	Public recognition
Stamps	Stickers Certificates	Letters home
Send to colleague	Send to phase coodinator / HT	Choosing time
Individual rewards	Class rewards Posts of responsibility	
Individual 'Good books'	Class 'Good Book' School Council Rep	

Others:

4)   What routines / procedures do you use for avoiding difficulties?

5)   What activities do you use for raising self-esteem / confidence / self-awareness etc

Circle work	Developing the 'language of feelings'	
Listening skills	Role-play	Assertiveness skills
Sharing skills	'News'	Conflict resolution skills

Others:

from **Developing and Implementing a Whole-School Behaviour Policy**   eds. D. Clarke and A. Murray

How children can sort out their own difficulties

Children should be encouraged to take responsibility for sorting out their own conflicts. This means that adults must take responsibility for teaching them and modelling strategies for doing this, and for seeing that children carry them out and reach a successful conclusion. Children should be encouraged to be assertive, to express their feelings and to resolve conflict without resorting to violence, swearing or abuse. Many schools recognise the need to teach conflict resolution skills; the example below comes from Columbia School in Tower Hamlets.

Columbia School's strategy for resolving conflicts – The 3 steps

One person speaks

The others listen with no interruptions

They are encouraged to maintain eye-contact

Each child has a turn to say:

1) *What the other(s) has done to upset them*

2) *How they feel about it*

3) *What they would like to happen in future*

No-one is allowed to interrupt or argue.

They go on taking turns until everyone has finished

The adult is there as a referee, not as part of the discussion. S/he makes sure that turns are taken, that children stick to the three steps, that they listen to each other and maintain eye-contact.

If the children cannot resolve the conflict after a reasonable time, then the adult can decide to make a judgement and take appropriate action.

Older pupils have started to add a 4th step: *Why did you do it?*

And more recently they have added a 5th: *'Shake hands and apologise'*

Children need to have the opportunity to identify the feelings connected to what has happened to them. Failure to allow for this process frequently means that the feelings get *acted out*. Having been able to acknowledge, and have acknowledged, the feelings involved, it seems easier for the pupils to take on the rational needs of the situation. It also makes it more likely that the 4th and 5th steps work. Trying to do these other steps before the other three tends to result in further argument and conflict rather than resolution. Obviously, this process cannot replace staff input in situations of serious conflict.

Intrinsic in this process is the idea that it is OK to feel angry, frustrated, irritated or upset, but not OK to act it out, ie behave badly or unpleasantly.

from **Developing and implementing a Whole-School Behaviour Policy** eds. D. Clarke and A. Murray

Incident Record / Referral Form

Referred to:

Name

Class

Teacher

Date

What I did

What rule I broke

Why I did it

What I can do to make it better

Teacher's comments

Student's signature

Teacher's signature

from Developing and Implementing a Whole-School Behaviour Policy   eds. D. Clarke and A. Murray

Welcome to
Rosendale Junior School

When you have filled this booklet in, Ms Edwards will sign it and you can take it home

My class is:

My teacher is called:

My Welcome Friends are:

I can bring to school:

I must not bring to school:

If I have a problem I should:

The school rules are:

1)

2)

3)

4)

5)

6)

Nobody is allowed to change playgrounds at playtimes.

I can play football in: _____ playground

I can play with a small ball in: _____ playground

I must go to for my lunch to:

I can only wear my hat in the:

My shoes must not have:

from **Developing and Implementing a Whole-School Behaviour Policy**   eds. D. Clarke and A. Murray   Designed by Su Edwards and Don Clarke

When I am in school I should move about:

If I bring money I must:

If anyone is unkind I should:

If I am being bullied I should:

Pupil signature:

Parent signature:

Headteacher:

My class rules are:

1)

2)

3)

4)

5)

6)

My PE day is: *and I must bring:*

My games day is: *and I must bring:*

My PE bag should go:

My coat should go:

Example of an 'Induction Booklet'

from **Developing and Implementing a Whole-School Behaviour Policy**   eds. D. Clarke and A. Murray

ACTIVITIES to promote reflection and discussion on behavioural issues

Formulate the ideas into sets of rules for the classroom / outside the classroom

Design posters to remind people of the different rules. These could be displayed in the classroom or around the school. The best could be laminated.

Write down the ideas generated

Draw a picture to illustrate one of the ideas.

The best could illustrate the Policy

Discuss in pairs or small groups:

What we *do* like people doing in the classroom

What we *don't* like people doing in the classroom

and / or

What we *do* like people doing in the playground

What we *don't* like people doing in the playground

Develop the ideas in role-play:

eg Making friends

Dealing with difficult situations

Using assertiveness skills

In Circle Time

Have rounds starting with:

....was friendly to me when ...

or

I didn't like it when someone ....

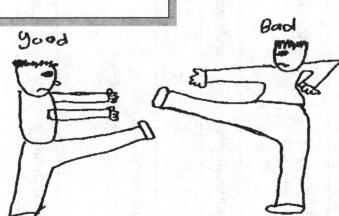

from **Developing and Implementing a Whole-School Behaviour Policy**   eds. D. Clarke and A. Murray

Two staff activities that focus on the feelings involved in the classroom – an aspect of 'Why dealing with difficult behaviour can be difficult'

These two activities are aimed at staff wishing to explore some of the feelings behind pupils' misbehaviour as well as behind their own responses to managing it in the classroom. Teachers usually enjoy the recognition of these (and other) feelings and usually relish the opportunity to talk about the incidents out of which they arose.

There is frequently a connection (and often a similarity) between how pupils feel and how teachers feel in their respective roles in the classroom.

Identifying legitimate ways for pupils to acknowledge some of their feelings can be an important activity for staff to undertake. Feelings may not necessarily change WHAT a person does, but it is likely to alter HOW they go about things.

Having one's own feelings recognised and acknowledged is often an important step in being sensitive to the feelings and perceptions of others.

Activity 1 – Pupil feelings:

In pairs or small groups, identify organisational factors or practice which which might trigger-off or exacerbate the following *feelings in pupils*?

> ***boredom   aggression   low self-esteem***
>
> ***confusion   powerlessness   frustration   fear***
>
> ***anxiety   insecurity   discouragement***

Consider what kinds of behaviours might result from these feelings?

Identify organisational factors or practice which might *minimise* these feelings or their repercussions.

Pairs or groups feedback to whole staff.

Activity 2 – Staff feelings:

These are feelings that teachers report having experienced when dealing with difficult behaviour. How many are you familiar with?

> ***discouraged   frustrated   intimidated***
>
> ***challenged   confused   deskilled   powerless***
>
> ***anxious   wanting to kill and maim***
>
> ***being out of control   panicy   vulnerable***

Brainstorm existing organisational factors or practice which might exacerbate or minimise these feelings or their repercussions.

Developing Positive Rules with Secondary Students
Teacher's notes for activity

AIM

The aim is to involve the students in the formulation of school rules. This may encourage them to take some ownership of the rules and hold then in higher regard. Meaningful rules have to be enforceable and have to be enforced consistently. Teachers are responsible for holding the students accountable for their work and behaviour by applying a range of consequences. If we wish to encourage self-discipline then we should give the students an active role to play in the identification of their responsibilities.

PROCESS

The process is designed to actively involve the students. The accompanying student prompt sheet is intended to help the class agree a common set of **positive** rules.

There are two tasks:

Task 1: to develop a set of rules for the class

Task 2: to develop a set of rules for a) the corridor and b) the playground

Ideally, following the introduction by the teacher, the students should engage in the process by:

1 Individually drafting a set of approximately 5 rules following the prompt sheet guidelines;

2 In small groups of 2 – 4, compare rules and agree a set

3 Each group reports back their rules to the whole class and a common list is agreed

Depending on the class conditions and student maturity it may be possible to have half the class work on Task 1, while the other half work on Task 2, with everyone participating in Stage 3 for both tasks.

Similarly, depending on the class in question, the process may need to be broken down into shorter sessions, completing Stages 1 and 2 in one session (e.g. half a lesson) and carrying out Stage 3 in the next lesson.

It may be possible to use the School Council as a means of establishing the whole-school set of rules for the staff to consider. Each class could use their reps (or Student Council reps) to present their class rules and participate in the final whole-school drafting process.

Designed by Bob Minter and Fiona Stephen

Positive Rules – *Student Sheet*

Task 1: Write a set of class rules that would help to make a classroom that you would like to work in.

Guidelines:

Remember the rules have to protect the rights that people have in school:

1. Teachers have the **right to teach**   2. Students have the **right to learn**

So, a rule like: 'We can make as much noise as we like' wouldn't be any use in a classroom although it might be OK for a party (if the neighbours were out).

The rules have to say what **should be happening** rather than banning things that **shouldn't be happening**.

So, *'We will treat each other with respect'* is better than *'No cussing'*.

Apart from trying to protect people's rights, the rules can also say what we expect from each other.

Example 1:   Pupils expect teachers to be fair and consistent, and to prepare work for them.

Example 2:   Teachers expect pupils to come to class prepared to do the work that will help them learn.

Expectations should be reasonable.

So, *'We must bring a laptop computer to every lesson'*

is an unreasonable rule, but:

 'We will bring the right equipment (pens, books etc) to lessons' is OK.

While some lessons like Drama or CDT have special additional rules, the ones we are going to write are general classroom rules of behaviour.

Rules should cover:
- *Noise level*
- *The way people treat each other*
- *Being prepared for lessons*
- *Movement in class*
- *Sorting out arguments*

Task 2: Write a set of rules for how pupils should behave:
     a) in the corridors   b) in the playground

Guidelines: These rules are bound to be different in some ways from the classroom rules. It's only necessary to have one or two rules for the corridors. Rules for the playground are very important because there might not be many teachers around.

Designed by Bob Minter and Fiona Stephen

Staff activity: Levels of behaviour and response

Fill in each space with the appropriate behaviours or responses

	Level 1	Level 2	Level 3	Exit-from-room
Behaviours				
Consequences / responses				

Behaviour that is low-level and part of general classroom management skills

Behaviour that requires a consequence either because of its intensity or frequency

Behaviours that require the deferred involvement of senior staff because of intensity or frequency

Behaviours that require the immediate removal from the classroom, to be followed up later by class teacher

from **Developing and Implementing a Whole-School Behaviour Policy**   eds. D. Clarke and A. Murray